MW00626002

TAPPING TO
RECLAIM YOU

How to Reignite your Passion,
Power and Purpose in 30 Days

SALLY THIBAULT

Copyright © Sally Thibault 2016
First print edition published in Australia 2016
eBook edition published in Australia 2016
Wisemothers Publishing
P O Box 1622, Oxenford
Australia 4210

www.sallythibault.com.au

All rights reserved. No part of this publication may be reproduced, stored in a retrieval system or transmitted in any form or by any means, electronic, mechanical, photocopying, recording or otherwise without the prior permission of both the copyright owner and the publisher of this book

National Library of Australia Cataloguing-in-Publication entry:
Thibault, Sally
Tapping to Reclaim You – How To Reignite Your Passion, Power and Purpose in 30 Days
Dewey No: 158.1
ISBN 978-0-9807374-4-8

Subjects:
1. Thibault, Sally
2. Tapping - Using tapping to heal life issues in the lives of women.
3. Case Studies of Transformation - Follows women through discovering their negative patterns, to the clearing and transformation of operating from their true self.
4. Self-actualization – Teaching women how to become the whole person they want to be by releasing old patterns and blockages (Psychology).

Editing & layout: www.bevryanpublishing.com

Book cover design: Rebecca Giovenco Photographer: Louise Williams at Emotive Images

DISCLAIMER
The author of this book does not dispense medical advice or prescribe the use of any technique as a form of treatment for physical, emotional or medical problems without the advice of a physician, either directly or indirectly. The intent of the author is only to offer information of a general nature to help you in your quest for emotional and spiritual wellbeing.
For the privacy of clients - most names, times, dates and some circumstances shared in this book have been changed. All suggestions in the book are educational in nature and for the reader's own self-improvement.

While the author is an experienced and certified EFT practitioner and Professional Counsellor, she is not a licensed healthcare provider and does not make any warranty or guarantee regarding the personal use of EFT (Tapping). In the event you use any of the information in this book for yourself or your clients, the author and publisher assume no responsibility for your actions or outcome.

To my children
David, Alissa, and Caitlin:

You are the reason I do this work
to clear the limitations within me and
release the patterns of the past
so you are free to live your very best lives.

Contents

Foreword

You have in your hands the most comprehensive, life changing, practical tool you may ever read in your life. I don't write this lightly – I have probably read just about everything out there, in my own quest to let go of old patterns, limiting beliefs, and feelings and behaviors that belong in the past. I have always been an impatient person – I want things done yesterday, mostly because there is so much more I can do tomorrow! When I struck the tool Sally teaches you in this book, I knew the planets had aligned to give me a tool that acted quickly, at deep unconscious levels, and lasted over time (permanently in most cases). I benefitted, my clients changed radically, and I started to research this tool at a clinical trial level in 2008 (see http://works.bepress.com/peta_stapleton/). The results have been outstanding and long lasting in all our clinical trials – for weight/food issues, depression, academic fears and worries, anxiety, chronic pain and more.

EFT (Emotional Freedom Techniques) or Tapping as it is commonly known, is a revolutionary self-help technique which combines eastern philosophies with modern day cognitive psychology. The act of tapping with two fingers on acupressure points on the body, while acknowledging your current state (feeling, belief, behavior, even pain) might seem a little strange to some, but the individual elements have been working for decades. Acupuncture has thousands of studies behind it now, and cognitive therapies have decades. This is first time they have been blended into one approach – a new wave or frontier for clients. The good news is there are no acupuncture needles in sight!

Sally Thibault has become an amazing and very close friend in her tapping journey – you will read and laugh about how we met in the first chapter. She is one of the most intuitive, centered, mindful EFT practitioner I have had the pleasure to have in my life. Whenever I run my own courses, it is Sally I invite to join as my peer. This book Sally has put together, which outlines her own journey, but more importantly gives you the reader the gift of EFT, is truly remarkable.

Sally has been able to drill down and outline the most common and often overlooked core issues that happen for people – and then offer tapping scripts with the actual words to say, in order to change. When people first come to tapping, they sometimes worry that they might not be saying the *right* words or don't know where to start. This book changes that as Sally has already outlined the tapping statements, the reminder phrases, and the plan you need to change any uncomfortable state you desire. As I said earlier, I have not come across such a comprehensive tapping guide to date – and I have read them all. This book will literally change your life.

The research about EFT has been growing for a decade now. We understand it to profoundly and quickly affect the part of the brain which sends out the stress response – which is why you can be in a state of complete overwhelm, anger, distress, fear (and so on) and after tapping for just a few minutes, feel considerably calmer. This is a surprise to many people as we often believe therapy or any intervention 'should' take a long time (especially if we have had our problem for a long time as well). Granted, we all have different internal senses of time, and some of us want things to take a little longer, and the brilliance of tapping is that you can take as long, or as little time as you like. The new wave of therapies in psychology are beginning to realize that change does not have to take a very long time – in fact the brain learns very quickly. Think of a child learning to walk. They might stand and wobble, then fall and crawl. But they stand soon after and attempt a step. Then they might fall.

They don't stand, fall over and think, 'That didn't work. I won't try that again.' Any parent will know that the skills learnt in early childhood happen very quickly! They walk before you know it!

Our brains are still like that. Neuroplasticity has shown us that we don't have fixed, rigid brains after our childhood years, never to learn again. We actually have malleable, flexible and extremely plastic brains which can learn new things, and unlearn old ones, very quickly. You just need the right tools to do it. Tapping is one of those tools.

I hope you enjoy this book as much as I have. I was introduced to tapping over 15 years ago now, in my quest for better therapeutic skills for my clients. Along the way I benefitted enormously and changed my own life. Sally has pulled together the most important elements you need to know, and you will truly appreciate the transparency with which she has shared exactly what you need to do.

Enjoy your journey! You were born with this amazing ability to know exactly what you are meant to be doing. If you haven't yet worked that out, tapping may be the key to unlock your own potential and Reclaim You!!

Dr. Peta Stapleton
Clinical and Health Psychologist
World Researcher in Emotional Freedom Techniques
www.petastapleton.com

Introduction

John Lennon once said, "Life is what happens while you are busy making other plans."

In reflection of my life, I see that has been entirely the outcome.

I have learned over the years that even though I believed I had a plan, my intuition and guidance from a *Source far greater than me* had other plans.

In this book, I will share some of that story, but mostly what I have come to believe is one of the greatest Energy Psychology techniques I have ever come across. The amazing, now evidence-based technique, known as tapping.

Since tapping has entered my life, I have experienced the most profound shifts. In fact I feel as if in my late 50s I am aging backwards. This technique has not only had a profound effect on my life, allowing me to experience more joy, more energy, more freedom, and more understanding of myself, but I have now been able to share it with hundreds of clients.

I have watched as clients have appeared younger and lighter, right before my eyes. I have facilitated the clearing of beliefs, emotions, and feelings that are so traumatic, yet within moments the pain and trauma of that memory changes, and a new understanding of the event becomes reality.

It is as if they have discovered who they are for the very first time, able to release the pain and emotion with a greater understanding of how their lives have unfolded because of that event.

Many times they have been able to move to a place where they are finally able to forgive the person or event that caused the trauma. At the same time, they are able to forgive the way in which the pattern that developed from the trauma has played itself out in their lives.

It is an amazing thing.

In this book I share with you a little of my story and many of my clients' stories. Each of us discovering how to *reclaim* ourselves, using the technique of tapping, to reignite the passion, power, and purpose in our lives, physically, emotionally, and spiritually.

I thank my clients for their faith in me. But also, as we know in the tapping world, often times their story is also mine. So their willingness to release beliefs, emotions, feelings, and patterns in their lives has allowed me to do so as well.

How my Tapping Story Began

There is very seldom a time in your life when something comes along that changes your perception of yourself so dramatically, that you have difficulty remembering who you were before it, yet you can remember the moment and just know that you were changed forever.

That happened to me. June 2013, when a friend of mine introduced me to tapping.

That day, in less than half an hour, I was changed, and it began a journey that opened up a world of possibilities that I could never have imagined.

This simple, rather odd looking technique, where you *tap* on various points of your face and upper body, while saying how you really feel. A technique that can shift deep seated, core beliefs that create patterns in your life which hold you back from experiencing the truest essence of you.

This book is about my journey and the journey of many of my clients, and how to *reclaim* the essence of who we really are.

One thing I have learned on this journey is that we are all born with the knowledge we need to create success, love, and happiness in our lives. We enter this physical life knowing how to love and bring joy to our world. We already have a deep inner connection to what we know to be true, even for what we will eventually do in our lives.

In fact, from the age of about two or three years old, you can often see a child's personality develop and the future unfold, by just watching that child play on their own.

A child left to play in their own imaginary world will play out what they love, often talking to themselves, or to other invisible individuals, and you can often see the beginnings of future careers. The connection to their true inner world is strong and beautiful.

But as we grow, events, people, or words said to us begin to create and disrupt that connection, creating doubt about what we believe is possible. Those doubts and subsequent beliefs create patterns which change our story. As the patterns become more ingrained, it becomes our truth. We begin to believe what is reflected back to us.

However, we can *reclaim* that true essence of ourselves. Through the power of tapping, I have seen both for me, and for many of my clients, an awakening and a return to self. The awakening often comes with incredible emotion, as the realization dawns that many times the patterns of our lives were not our truest self; instead, we have just been playing out that which we believed to be true!

This modality of tapping is so powerful. As you release the patterns that no longer serve you, you are free to reignite the passion, power and purpose within you – without the limitations that have impacted on what you believed possible in the past. You are free to create a whole new definition of yourself and your story. It is incredibly exciting. That at any time, you can simply rewrite your own story!

I am living proof that this process can reverse the aging clock and create more passion, power, and purpose than I believed possible. I see it over and over again for my clients as well. Many clients rediscovering their passion for a business idea, and starting a business that they had once dreamed of but didn't believe possible; releasing weight that no longer serves them; finding the courage and strength to leave a relationship that was co-dependent and instead attract their soul mate into their lives. I have seen clients mend broken relationships with parents, siblings, or children, and create a relationship of far greater meaning and love.

Most of all, I have come to understand how each and every belief, thought, and feeling in our lives stems from our reaction to an event, word, or person from our past, and how you can change the intensity of that emotion so it no longer dominates your life in a negative way.

You can change the influence of your past, to create a new future that you design.

Success is not *changing* who we are; it is *reclaiming* who we are. Our gifts, our dreams, and our passions that we were born with.

For me this awakening led me to a new career. A career where I watch women change before my eyes. Able to release painful emotions that have profoundly impacted on their lives. Women who have released years of pain of sexual abuse, domestic violence, physical and emotional bullying that has masked itself in patterns of self-sabotage. Women who always knew there was a *something* that held them back from being successful, but just couldn't figure it out.

It is awe-inspiring to witness so many women rediscover their own inner passion, power, and wisdom and *reclaim* their body and their lives.

I truly believe that this is the time of the *wise woman*. The woman who has spent the most part of the last few decades raising children, and caring for others. Who is now looking forward to the next chapter of her life – the chapter that is all about *her* time.

I invite you to read my personal story and the stories of clients. (Most names and some identifiable places or dates have been changed to protect their privacy.) Throughout this book, you will discover how many times releasing beliefs and patterns that are so close to you they have become your best friend, can be challenging. But once they are gone, the freedom is simply extraordinary.

At the end of each chapter is a tapping script, the one that I have created for each of the client stories. While tapping to scripts is not the most powerful way to release emotional issues, it can help to lower the intensity of the stress or anxiety you may feel. Working with a certified and experienced EFT practitioner is the most powerful way to help you release the patterns that are holding you back.

Welcome to the journey of *Reclaiming You*. I look forward to being with you over the next 30 days as you rediscover the *real* you.

Much love,
Sally xo

CHAPTER 1

My Story

In April 2013, I had the most wonderful experience of heading to San Diego for a three-day conference with Facebook expert Mari Smith. During the course of the weekend, we were fortunate to spend some time experiencing an enlightening presentation by the beautiful Esperanza Universal.

At one stage during her presentation, she singled me out to say, "You have a light that shines. That light will be a powerful force and you will change people's lives because of it." At the time, I didn't realize how powerful that light would eventually be, and it wasn't until many months later that the direction of my life changed, and I finally understood what she meant.

This is my story.

It had been a tough few months for Gerry and me. I was struggling to find speaking engagements to promote the work I was doing in autism, after the release of my first book.

The book was released in 2010, and tells the story of our family's journey following our son's diagnosis of Asperger's Syndrome.

I was fortunate to have received some great press coverage, which included appearing on two national TV shows and numerous radio and newspaper interviews. From there stemmed many opportunities to speak at conferences and professional development days for medical practitioners, counselors, teachers, and parents about the impact that autism can have on a family. It had been a very busy and fulfilling few years, but I was starting to feel that my work in autism was no longer the work I was supposed to be doing.

The problem was, it wasn't really the work; it was me. I just didn't *feel* I was enough. Even appearing on national TV and being recognized as an expert in the field wasn't enough to make me feel successful.

Some days were great, especially when I was working with people whose lives were directly impacted by autism, but I would always come away feeling something was missing.

Even though I always received great feedback and testimonials from clients I worked with and from audience participants, there was always a thought in the back of my mind that somehow I wasn't good enough, wasn't worthy enough, or educated enough.

I felt inadequate and insignificant. I then started having huge doubts about my ability to work with others, or to make a sustainable career from the work I was doing.

In late 2012, I joined a fabulous online international business community facilitated by the effervescent, fabulous Mari Smith. Mari, at the time, launched her *Business and Beyond Club*, helping business owners from all over the world come together to learn not only about social media and business, but also personal development techniques.

Every Wednesday at 4am, I would be on the call with Mari in the US, as she set us tasks to complete in the week ahead. Part of this was being set up in accountability groups. Each week, four of us would get together on Skype to discuss problems and issues we faced with our tasks, celebrate our achievements, and generally just keep each other accountable.

During the time at the conference, I also had the opportunity to attend the first *Social Media Marketing World* event, which ran just after Mari's workshop. It opened my eyes to the amazing possibilities that now existed in social media.

I came home fired up and ready to create a career in social media. It was very short lived. I'll admit I do love social media, but I soon realized it was not a passion!

So by the June of that year, I was lost. I wasn't quite sure where to head next.

To top it all off, my eldest son and youngest daughter both left home within two weeks of each other. My son moved to Montreal to live with his girlfriend, and my daughter was offered a position as the Head of Dance at a summer camp in the US. Our middle daughter had left home at 18 to live on campus at her university, and had moved many times for her career, but never more than one hour's plane trip away.

Gosh, talk about feelings of inadequacy. Not only was I being challenged by what I was going to do with my life, but at the same time we were becoming empty nesters! And not just any ordinary empty nesters – two of our children were heading thousands of miles away! No coming home for Sunday lunch.

Those few weeks were really tough and every time I thought of the two of them leaving my eyes would fill with tears. We had always told our kids from a very early age that they had to travel and experience the world before they settled down. Both Gerry and I had travelled; in fact, that is how we met. But I didn't think they would listen to me – they certainly didn't listen when I asked them to clean their rooms!

So here I was. That time in my life that everyone talked about, but I didn't think would happen. All our children were leaving home.

Suddenly, after 30 years of raising children, that reality changed for good within two short weeks

That began the internal questioning.

Who was I? Who was I, without the *full-time mother* label? Our world no longer revolved around school, dance, soccer, and work. There were no more, "Mum you will never guess what happened today?" conversations that took place spontaneously. There were no more, "Bye Mum, I will let you know if I am coming home for dinner." No messy kitchens, no laundry baskets overflowing, or wet towels on the bedroom floor. (I wasn't so upset about that part!)

But who did I become, now that child raising, mentoring, and caring for children was at an end?

There is a strange mourning that goes on when the last child leaves home; quite honestly I never thought I would experience it. Perhaps I just never thought the day would come.

But here it was and it was like somebody turned the energy off in the house. One minute our house was full of bubbling, crashing, noisy energy, and the next minute it was silent.

For a few weeks, the silence in the house was almost deafening. So I just kept busy, trying to fill the void made by our children leaving. Then, one Friday night, Gerry and I were sitting in the living room. A glass of wine in hand, we had enjoyed a plate of antipasto. After talking for hours, we realized it was after 8pm. We looked at each other and I said, "Actually this empty-nester thing isn't so bad after all!"

But now what?

The next week, on my weekly accountability call, one of my accountability buddies, Susan Beebe, who resides in the US, offered to do a tapping session for both Gerry and me.

I had heard of tapping before, but to tell the truth, I thought it looked a bit silly. Besides, how could tapping on parts of your face and upper body have anything to do with releasing stress?

I had come across tapping in 2009, seeing the marketing for the World Tapping Summit. But I was always skeptical with therapies that looked too *new-agey,* without some evidence to back it all up.

Raising a child on the autism spectrum had made me extremely skeptical about anything that was not proven. In our time we had come across, and wanted to believe in, so many alternative therapies that offered the world and delivered nothing.

We believe in alternative therapies: homeopathy, naturopathy, acupuncture, etc. But after years of disappointment and money spent, I'm now skeptical of anything that is without some solid foundation.

But Susan was insistent that tapping was one of the modalities that had helped her in her business, and talking to her each week, I could tell that something was certainly working. Her business, and her personal life, were going from strength to strength.

On this particular day, both Gerry and I were at a real stalemate in our businesses. He had been working on a property contract for months. It was a brilliant opportunity for development, but he just couldn't find a buyer for it. I hadn't had a speaking engagement for months. I had sent out many proposals, but nothing was coming together. It was after voicing some frustration on our weekly call that Susan offered to do a tapping session for us.

We were set up on Skype and she explained the process of tapping – how it worked, the acupressure points, and the setup statements. She asked a few questions about what was going on for us and began the tapping.

We wanted to focus on the subject of money and why it seemed we were always struggling for money. We were by no means destitute, but there always seemed to be some negative energy around it.

She asked us to measure the level of intensity, stress, or emotion around our current money issues. That was easy – the stress levels were a high level ten!

So we began the process. I was surprised at how much she focused on the negative; I was so used to using affirmations. It was quite confronting to actually say how you really felt.

After a couple of rounds of tapping on *this stress of money,* she asked us both to recall our earliest memory of money. I started to giggle as I recalled my mother's favorite saying, "You will just have to wait for our ship to come in!" To this day, I can still see myself as a little girl standing on the shore of Port Phillip Bay in Victoria, looking at all the container ships trying to figure out which ship was ours.

When she asked what the level of intensity of the memory was, again, it was quite high. I truly believed that you couldn't receive money until you waited your turn. Now that was an interesting aha!

Again, after a couple of rounds of tapping on that image, I was very aware of it becoming less intense.

Susan rechecked both levels before we finished, and I was really amazed at how the stress had dissipated.

What I wasn't prepared for was what happened next.

Within two hours of our tapping session I received an email from a conference organizer. Her keynote speaker had pulled out due to illness and she asked if I was available at such short notice. After confirming some of the logistics, she transferred a deposit straight into my account and booked the airfares that afternoon.

The next day, Gerry received a call from a client, who offered a cash contract on the property he had been working on for months!

Coincidence? When something happens once perhaps, but twice? There was something to this tapping thing and I was going to find out what it was.

I wanted to know more, so Susan directed me the EFT Universe website and I found the workshop page.

I couldn't believe what I read. There was an EFT training coming up in three weeks in Brisbane! I later found out there was only one EFT Universe trainer in Australia at the time and she would be holding the event on the only weekend I had free that entire month.

The coincidences didn't end there. Her surname is the same as my maiden name, and she lived about five minutes away from my sisters in Melbourne!

So I booked in for both the Level 1 and Level 2 workshops and started researching.

I wanted to know everything about the modality. I was thrilled and surprised to discover how much research and evidence there was supporting tapping. I knew that this was the group I wanted to learn more from; my skeptical, autism parent self being very satisfied.

As I was researching, I came across the name of a university professor on the Gold Coast, Dr. Peta Stapleton, who had led a large trial on the impact of tapping on food cravings. My interest was piqued. As a former fitness instructor and seminar presenter, before my son was diagnosed, I had worked with women to teach them how to lose weight permanently through intuitive eating.

I had written a manuscript many years before called *Fit, Fabulous and Free, the Art of Losing Weight Permanently*. It was in the garage somewhere, along with a couple of publisher rejection letters. It was my first foray into being an author, thwarted by particularly bad writing.

I began to read Dr. Stapleton's research and set out to learn more about her. I discovered she was now at Bond University – literally 30 minutes from our home.

Each morning I tried to summon up enough courage to write Dr. Stapleton an email. But then I would stop and think – *She will think I am crazy; she probably gets thousands of emails a day!* I never sent it.

At the time, I was still working in the field of autism and had been approached by a university to become a guest lecturer. I spoke to the Head of Department about implementing tapping into the program to show teachers a way to calm anxiety in children, and he was open to the idea.

The day for the EFT training came and I was very excited. I'd done all the research I could – read books, articles, and watched hundreds of videos. I was ready to discover more about this modality.

However, I misjudged the time it would take for me to walk from the train station to the event itself, so I arrived about ten minutes late.

I walked into the room, which was set up in a U-shape, and took a spot at the front. It was a little like church – all the back seats had gone and only the seats at the very front were still free.

As I sat down, I was asked to introduce myself and then subsequently each participant followed, about 12 participants in all. It was interesting to hear everybody's background and reasons for being there – hypnotherapists, counselors, and those just interested in learning more about EFT.

There was a small blonde woman sitting on the other side of the room and I kept thinking that I knew her from somewhere. As her turn came to introduce herself, she said, "Hi everyone, my name is Dr. Peta Stapleton." I couldn't believe it – I suddenly burst out with, "Oh my god, I have been stalking you!" Everybody laughed and then I thought, *she is going to think I am an idiot!*

The training over the four days was really intense, but I just loved it.

At the end of the second day, we were asked us to bring a food that we wanted to give up. I couldn't think of anything that had a particular hold on me, and then I remembered – *Twisties*. I didn't buy them because once I started eating them, I would eat the whole packet.

So the next day we all had a turn at tapping on this food craving. I opened the pack of *Twisties, yum!* I loved the cheesy smell. Peta asked us to taste one. *Yum*, again I thought, *I love the crunch, the salty taste, and that powerful cheesy taste*.

We tapped on a few rounds of what we loved about it.

Then she asked us to eat it again; for some reason, I couldn't taste the cheesiness as strongly. We tapped on another round.

Peta asked us to smell and taste the food again – *YUK!* Suddenly I couldn't taste the cheese anymore. Instead, it tasted like chemicals and actually made me feel quite nauseous.

I couldn't even have the food on the desk in front of me; I had to throw it in the bin.

I sat looking at the full packet in the bin; even throwing the food away was a step forward. I had grown up in a family where throwing out food was considered extremely wasteful.

At this moment, I knew I had found what I wanted to do for the rest of my life.

On the last day, we were asked for a volunteer to show a particular technique and without hesitating – or believing that I had any *real* issues – I volunteered for the demonstration.

Within five minutes, I was tapping on all the grief, emotions, sadness, and fears of raising a child on the autism spectrum – all those issues that I had thought I had dealt with, but suddenly realized I had only ignored.

It was a very emotional session and even touched on some past life issues. I felt so different, so light and joyful. Something major had shifted.

That next week, I flew to Victoria to present at an autism conference, talking about bullying and how it impacted on children living with autism.

The presentation room was packed and the theme of the presentation was the fact that we were mostly focused on the prevention of bullying, but not on the emotional impact of bullying on the children. I believe we must heal the pain of bullying for children to enable them to stop the pattern of bullying from continuing, especially for those living on the autism spectrum.

I talked a little bit about tapping, but really didn't know that much about it at that stage, and was by no means an expert. I did mention that I had come across a modality that I felt could reduce the emotional impact of bullying, and perhaps it was something that parents might want to research for themselves.

After the presentation, I was swamped with questions about tapping and organized a demonstration for those interested.

The response was amazing – I conducted 15-minute sessions for 18 people and even though I was just a newcomer to tapping, I could see that it had some immediate impact on some of the people who wanted to experience it. From that moment, I was hooked.

The next week I arranged to meet Peta and after chatting for a couple of hours, I was enthralled by her research, her insight into EFT, and the many ways in which it could be used.

I asked her about tapping and money, as it seemed to be something that really shifted for me. Her response was that there were no Australian practitioners focusing on that area at that time.

Okay, well then I will be that person! (One of the things I released by tapping was my need to be perfect!)

I was due to give a presentation on *stress* at a networking event the following week. So I phoned the organizer and asked if I could do a presentation on *tapping, stress, and money*. She was most gracious in agreeing.

I created a power point presentation, read all I could on *tapping* and *money,* and presented to a packed room. From that presentation, eight people signed up to work with me over the next month.

It was great. I loved it and the women I worked with began to create change in their lives, stepping out of marriages that were not working, healing their own money blockages, and starting to lose weight.

I was enjoying the mentoring aspect and while I still was doing some work in the autism field, I could feel that coming to an end.

My son was now 29, and was living and working overseas and moving on with his life. In November of that year, Gerry and I sat down and had a long conversation. I felt that while I continued to work in the field of autism, our son was tied to me. Everybody wanted to know about him and I felt it wasn't fair. This was his life now. I needed to unravel the tangle, and let him be free to live his own life, without being tied to his mother's work.

I had a few more autism commitments to complete, but I knew it was time to wrap it up. I approached a wonderful member of our autism community about taking over the very active Facebook page *Asperger's Parent Connect* that I had created, which she graciously and enthusiastically accepted.

I spoke at numerous networking events over the next six months, each and every time picking up new clients. Peta and I decided to host an event together on *tapping* and *money*. She was looking forward to presenting on something different, and I felt I had enough data to host and present at a full day.

We were pleasantly surprised at the interest, and the presentation on the day was fabulous.

At the end, I asked those present if anybody would like to have a strategy session with me to see if and how I could help them. Fifteen people requested sessions!

From those sessions, six people committed to working with me over a six week period. Not one of them wanted to work on money issues. They all wanted to use tapping for weight loss!

The six-week program was wonderful and I again saw such massive, yet subtle shifts in the clients. They had come to me from a money seminar and wanted to work on their weight issues, but there were common themes that became evident. Feeling unworthy, feeling unloved or unlovable, feeling unsupported, feeling invisible, feeling powerless, and feeling ignored.

Some seemed to attract money into their lives, but struggled with their weight; some attracted success easily, but struggled to attract the relationship they wanted. But for most people, it boiled down to these common themes.

Underlying all those feelings were beliefs that eventuated from certain events, people, or words of their past. Those feelings then changed what they believed about themselves and were then continually reinforced. In other words, they just kept attracting the same patterns into their lives, over and over again, because of what they now believed to be true. Our brain continually seeks ways to reaffirm what we believe is true about ourselves.

It's why we repeat the same pattern in our lives – over and over again!

It became very obvious that just working on *weight, money,* or *relationships* was never the issue. Rather, it was exploring and releasing the beliefs, patterns, and stories that kept repeating themselves and expressed themselves as issues of *weight, money,* or *relationship* challenges.

There was a block that seemed to be common amongst my clients, who were mostly in their mid to late 40s and 50s. The issue of believing they were *worthy* of success in *all* areas of their lives. It was almost as if there was some internal bargaining going on – that they were not *worthy of having it all* and they simply played that belief out as if they were actors in somebody else's play!

Many simply did not believe they could experience success in every facet of their lives. In fact they would often sabotage themselves before even starting, or whenever they got close to success. Losing weight, and then putting it all back on again. Dreaming of creating their own business, but never feeling confident to start. Or creating success in their career, but struggling to find a partner to support them.

It is as if, as women, we don't believe we can actually have happiness and success in all areas of our lives, all at the same time!

During each and every program, no matter how it started out, the same issues arose.

Many clients had lost the memory of *who* they were; years of trauma, pain, abuse, neglect, bullying, judgment, or lack of unconditional love resulted in them forgetting the *who* they were meant to be.

It was then I began working and tapping with clients to *reclaim* who they were. Because it became so obvious that so many women believed that in order to be truly successful and powerful, lose weight, or attract the perfect partner, they had to *be* somebody different.

Nothing could be further from the truth. *Success is not changing who we are; it is reclaiming who we are.* The real us – the one before the events, people, or words changed what we believed we were capable or worthy of having.

It was then that I truly understood the work that I believed I was sent here to fulfill, and *Tapping to Reclaim You* was born.

I invite you to join with me, as I take you through the steps I use to create success in my life, and to help clients create it in theirs, simply *by not changing who you are – but reclaiming who you really are!*

CHAPTER 2

So What is This Tapping Thing?

Tapping, more formally referred to as EFT – *Emotional Freedom Techniques* – is a powerful self-help modality. Tapping uses elements of Cognitive Behavioral Therapy and Exposure Therapy then combines them with fingertip tapping on nine acupuncture points around the face and upper part of the body.

Now widely practiced, EFT has over 60 clinical trials or peer-reviewed reports. The reports have demonstrated tapping's effectiveness for phobias, anxiety, depression, post-traumatic stress disorder, pain, food cravings, and more.

Tapping was originally developed by psychologist Dr. Roger Callahan, who discovered tapping while working with a patient with a severe water phobia.

One of his students, Gary Craig, began experimenting with tapping and simplified the procedure, which later became the version widely used today.

Clinical trials have shown that tapping is able to rapidly reduce the emotional impact of memories and incidents that trigger emotional distress.

It works by lowering cortisol levels. A randomized controlled study by Dr. Dawson Church and his team focused on changes to cortisol levels in 83 subjects. They were separated into three groups – one used EFT, another a conventional therapy, and the final group received no treatment.

The final group and the conventional therapy group showed only a 14% drop in cortisol over time. While the EFT group showed a 24% decrease in cortisol, with some experiencing up to 50% decrease.

It appears that once distress or stress is reduced or removed, the body can often rebalance itself, and accelerate healing.

My dear friend and colleague, Dr. Peta Stapleton, is one of the world's leading researchers into EFT for food cravings. In the world's first controlled study, 89 women between the ages of 31 and 56, who had a body mass index (BMI) in the obese range, took part in approximately two hours of tapping per week (just over 15 minutes a day), over eight weeks. Just by tapping (with no dieting) they lost an average of 8 kilos by the end of the study.

In July 2014, I was honored to be a part of a research trial looking into the impact of tapping for Year 10 students. The students reported that their level of stress and anxiety around study was significantly reduced by using the technique.

From that study, Dr. Stapleton and I have developed *Tapping for the Classroom* –www.tappingintheclassroom.com – a program specifically for teachers, school guidance officers, and psychologists.

How to Tap

While there are now many versions of tapping available, I prefer to use what is commonly known as Clinical EFT, simply because the majority of the studies mentioned before involve the use of this particular style.

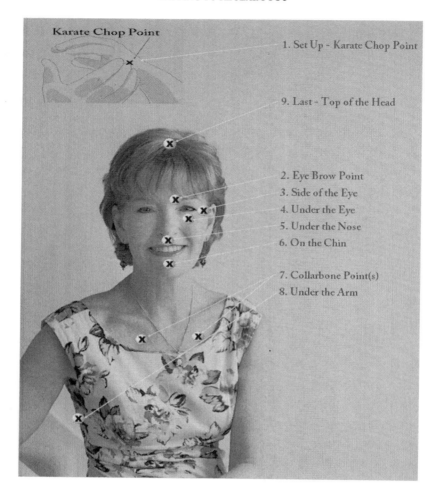

There are nine tapping points used in the clinical version of EFT.

1. **Karate Chop Point** – with three fingers, tap the side of your other hand where you would do a *karate chop*. In the book I refer to this as the ***Set-Up Statement*** as you'll see through the next chapters.

    The points then work in sequence (tapping on each point about 4 – 8 times).

32

2. **EB** means *Eyebrow Point* – where the hair of the eyebrow meets the nose.

3. **SE** means *Side of the Eye* – follow the bone around the eye socket and tap.

4. **UE** means *Under the Eye* – again follow the bone of the eye socket and tap under the eye, directly under the pupil.

5. **UN** means *Under the Nose* – the part of the face under the nose and above the lips.

6. **Chin** means *Chin Point* – the groove just below the lips, but above the chin bone itself.

7. **CB** means *Collar Bone Point* – find the *U shape* that connects your collar bone where it meets in the centre of your chest; drop down a little and you will feel the fleshy part on either side, just under the collar bone.

8. **UA** means *Under the Arm* – about four inches from the armpit, or where the bra strap would sit for a woman.

9. **TH** means *Top of the Head* – right in the centre of the skull.

You can tap with one hand, or both hands, and on whichever side is comfortable for you. In tapping there is no right or wrong – simply what feels right for you.

For more information, please see the range of tapping videos available on my website www.sallythibault.com.au

Telling the Truth and Being Specific

Tapping's great power, I believe, comes from our ability to connect to our own truth. All too often we are not encouraged to tell the truth about how we feel. We are encouraged to think positively, often ignoring our true emotions.

For many clients, *telling the truth* is often the first time they have actually voiced how they really felt about an issue – those beliefs, thoughts, and words buried deep within their subconscious. The ones that we don't often want to admit we have.

There is no political correctness in tapping – it is how *you* feel, what *you* think and nobody will judge you or try to sugar coat it for you. Whatever *you* feel, or say, is right for *you*! The quality of the words you use, getting as close as you can to how you are really feeling, will create a more powerful outcome.

As an example, if you want to tap to deal with your weight, rather than just saying, "Even though I don't like my weight the way it is," a more specific statement would be, "Even though the thought of putting on a bikini and walking onto the beach makes me feel so embarrassed, because I have gained 10 kilos and I just feel fat and I hate myself." That's the truth part. It doesn't make you right or wrong – it's just the truth for you.

People telling you to love yourself when you don't will not make you love yourself – no matter how many times you say it!

How to Use the Tapping Scripts

While many of the tapping scripts in this book are somewhat generalized, tapping is most powerful when you are as specific as you can be about how you are feeling, as in the example above.

The more specific you can be about the beliefs, thoughts, or feelings, the faster you will be able to release a pattern and change the way you experience life.

The following tapping scripts ask a series of questions before you begin tapping. The questions are important to try to gain clarity and get to the root cause of a feeling of discomfort.

Many people have lost the art of being in touch with their emotions. Whether that has been through conditioning – growing up in a family where emotion was considered a weakness;

or learning at a young age how to disconnect from your emotions, in order to feel safe. This can cause an emotional disconnect.

Our body will reflect what is going on for us emotionally, whether we like to believe it or not!

You may experience a headache if you are feeling stressed; a sore lower back if you are feeling unsupported; tiredness if you are overwhelmed. Many of the discomforts we feel may come from an emotion or a belief we have ignored.

The problem is that many people either put up with the discomfort or choose to take medication instead, rather than first examining if there is an emotional reason behind it.

Your body is like your early warning system. It lets you know when something isn't right, but many people have become disconnected from the *mind* that exists within their body.

Tapping helps you reconnect to the way your body feels, allowing you to become very adept at knowing when something doesn't feel right, and at the same time uncovering the reason for the pain, or the emotion you feel, and sometimes even healing it!

We always begin with a *Set-Up Statement*, tapping on the *Karate Chop* point. And we say the words, "Even though I have this issue, I deeply and completely accept myself and how I feel." In other words – even though you have this issue going on you are fine! It's just an issue, and you accept that this is how you feel!

Before tapping with any client, the first thing I ask is, "What emotion are you feeling?" and "Where in your body do you feel it?" When people first start tapping, some struggle with the concept of *finding the feeling*, but after a while they become attuned to their own bodies.

This is especially the case with stress. Stress comes in all forms and shows up in many ways in our body. A number of clients I work with will tell me they feel stress in their neck and shoulders, and fear and anxiety in their gut. When we begin to identify the reason for that stress or anxiety, tell the truth and tap on the reasons or emotions, the discomfort or pain often dissipates very quickly.

How Often do You Need to Tap?

Tapping is like exercise for your beliefs – a routine that forms part of your daily habits, just like exercise or meditation.

It is not a standalone practice, but a way of living. I suggest to clients to use tapping any time they have a disempowering thought or feeling, like those pesky negative thoughts that in tapping we refer to as *tail-enders*; the thoughts that are the *yeah right,* or *yes but* thoughts that flow through your mind every time you want to make a change in your life

Our beliefs about ourselves are supported by various aspects. Gary Craig referred to our issues as *Table tops,* supported by various aspects he called *Table legs.* The *Table legs* may be all sorts of events, words, or emotions from the past that combine to form a belief – the *Table top.*

What we believe to be true for us is supported by a core belief that may have, at its heart, an event/s, a person/people, or a word/s that caused us pain in the past. Until we deal with each one of those emotions, events, or issues, we will continue to recreate the same patterns in our lives that come from that belief.

For example, perhaps you always procrastinate when you have a big project or goal you want to achieve. You may procrastinate so much that you leave everything until the last minute and then experience a great deal of stress to eventually get it done. It doesn't matter how important the project is, or how badly you want to complete it, you always have trouble starting, and completing, the task without an enormous amount of stress or adrenalin to push you through.

When thinking about the project, words or thoughts such as *I always do this; I am just lazy,* or *maybe it won't be good enough,* or *close enough is good enough,* may continually run through your mind (the *Tail-enders*).

The way to change the habit is to not focus on the procrastination, but rather to examine what emotions, thoughts, or feelings cause you to procrastinate (the *Table legs*). Because the procrastination is a symptom of a belief you have about you, usually stemming from your reaction to a person/event or words from your past (the *Table top*).

Perhaps completing the task means that you will be successful and that feels scary for you. Perhaps there was an event in your past where you were successful and people challenged or criticized you. Perhaps there was a person in your past who told you that you were not worthy of success. Perhaps you were once told that you would never amount to anything in your life. Or perhaps all of them!

The procrastination is simply a way to keep you safe from experiencing the pain of the past. The thoughts that run through your mind reiterate what you believe to be true about yourself (*Tail-enders*). In order to totally overcome the habit of procrastination you need to find all the *aspects (Table legs)* that keep you continuing with that behavior and the belief that causes you to continue to repeat the pattern (*Table top*). Sometimes you can tap and release all the aspects in one go; sometimes it takes a little longer. But if you still do it – you haven't cleared it!

Nothing we do is ever random. There is always a reason behind all our behaviors – the good and the not so good. If you have a pattern or a habit that you want to change in your life you can. Simply by being mindful of your thoughts and feelings and tapping to uncover and release the cause of the belief in the first place.

Is it Magic?

I am not sure about calling tapping magic – but there are some outcomes that I have trouble explaining!

There are two things that seem to happen in tapping. One is a physiological impact and the other – well, perhaps it is magic after all!

The Physiological Part

Tapping appears to calm the emotional response to any disturbing event in our past, by deactivating the brain's arousal pathways.

The amygdala, hippocampus, and hypothalamus – part of the brain's limbic system – play a key role in processing our emotions. The hippocampus is responsible for the processing and storage of short term memory. The amygdala is responsible for emotions, moods, and other functions. Keeping us safe, by helping to stimulate our stress response – the *flight, fight, freeze, or faint* response. Our brain's hypothalamus also sends signals to our pituitary gland and adrenal glands to produce a stress hormone – cortisol. While cortisol is a natural hormone in our body, which helps get us moving and achieve what we need to do, when we experience high levels of stress, high levels of cortisol impact on our health and weight, and are responsible for the flight, fight, fear, and faint responses that overwhelm us when we are super stressed or anxious.

Memories stored in the amygdala stop us from moving past the pain and trauma of the past, instead causing us to relive the trauma over and over again, and then rewiring a new pattern that is designed to keep us safe, but trapped in the repeating pattern.

For instance, a fear of public speaking could stem from the time you fell over in the school playground and everybody laughed at you; anxiety and fear causing you to feel high levels of fear every time you are required to speak in public – reminding you that if you slip up, people might laugh at you.

A boyfriend breaking up with you when you were 13 years old may cause your fear response to go into overdrive every time you feel a relationship getting more serious; the fear or trauma of being rejected being responsible for you sabotaging any relationship before you get hurt again.

We are the sum total of all the trauma, fears, or emotions of our past, which are simply playing out as patterns in our present.

Tapping helps to calm our emotional responses to an event, then reduces the flight, fight, freeze, or faint response, allowing rational, wisdom based, calm thought to return. This helps to effectively clear trauma and emotion caused from experiences of your past, and to create new patterns to success for your new future!

The Magic Part

One of my favorite sayings is *In order for things to change, first I must change,* and in tapping, this is the absolute truth.

Many of my clients tell me that when they tap on something that drives them crazy about somebody else – magically that person seems to stop doing whatever it was that drove them crazy!

The issue is never about the other person. It is always about us. When we take 100% responsibility for our reactions, we can release the emotional intensity we have to the behaviors of others.

What we think and feel creates energy that reflects outwards from us and in doing so creates who, or what, we attract into our lives. Tapping on what we feel suddenly changes that.

What I have seen happen over and over again, however, is difficult to explain. I have worked with clients who are worried or upset about a child's behavior, then tap on how that behavior makes them feel and within days that child stops exhibiting that behavior! I have also had clients who have tapped on how a boss or a co-worker treats them that makes them feel stressed or frustrated – to then have that boss or co-worker suddenly treat them as if they were their best friend!

As we tap on how we feel about something, and shift the intensity of that feeling or emotion, we change. Our vibrational energy changes and lifts. When that happens, we change how we respond, and people change how they respond to us. I liken it to creating a void. When you change your way of exhibiting a certain energy, you change the dynamics of that energy field around you and something different has to fill the void. Ever walked into a room where people have been arguing – and you can just *feel* the tense energy in the room? Same thing happens with how you express your energy. When you change the way you feel about somebody or something – you change how they *feel* they need to respond to you – because they feel a different energy from you.

I found this with children living with autism. They have an uncanny way of responding to certain emotions from people, as they are highly sensitive. Many times they respond to people's stresses and energy – and surprisingly people tend to think it is about the child, without understanding that the child is responding to, and often overwhelmed by, the energy expressed by others!

When we accept and acknowledge that everything is energy, we can change how others react to us and how we react to others. If somebody shows up in your life who creates a negative response in you – instead of blaming, judging, or criticizing that person, simply ask yourself, "What is this person reflecting that I need to heal in me?" Usually they will remind you of a person, event, or words that were said to you in the past. By tapping on the memory and the feeling, you can change the entire energy of the interaction! How cool is that?

When you tap and clear the limiting beliefs and patterns, including how you respond to certain energy, it is as if the true magic of who you are, and what you are truly capable of experiencing, unfolds.

How to Use This Book

The intent of this book is to help you to reignite the passion, power, and purpose in your life, through this powerful modality of tapping, and at the same time, help you to release any limiting beliefs or patterns that are holding you back from expressing the real you.

The process works like this.

In the next chapter, I will ask you to create a *One-word theme* – a powerful process to help you to create clarity in your life.

Then, in Chapter 4, I will ask you to create an intention you want to focus on for the next 30 days, and create a plan of action to help you make that intention come to reality.

Then, in each following chapter, you will find tapping scripts to deal with any negative thoughts or beliefs that may arise after you set your intention.

These tapping scripts come from both my own experience and from stories of my clients. Each chapter has a theme, often with a story about how a client was able to release a limiting belief by understanding how the belief was created.

You can either work through each of the chapters, one after the other, or jump between them, depending on any negative thoughts, or events that may arise for you, as you go through the 30-day process.

Every day for 30 days, set aside time to tap. Ensure you keep a journal, or a list, of the beliefs you release and the changes that you experience.

Many people who tap experience a phenomenon called the *Apex effect*. When they tap on a specific memory or event, the intensity can reduce so dramatically that they forget they had any issue to begin with!

I have experienced this in my own tapping. I have been keeping a journal of my tapping for this reason. Sometimes I look back on a certain journal entry and can't believe I used to think that way! The change has been so subtle that I didn't even notice. Often times it's not a huge *AHA* awakening change, rather a particular issue that no longer impacts on me, or I just don't do something the way I used to. I notice this particularly after I have tapped to release an emotional attachment to a certain food. I just don't want it, crave it, or even think about that food any longer. It's not a conscious choice *to not* have it; I just don't think *to* have it! It was the reason one Christmas we had no chocolate in the house, as I just didn't even think to buy it – my children were horrified!

The Tapping Scripts

In each tapping script, I will ask you to identify the emotion or feeling and to be as accurate as you can. Then after identifying *what* you feel, to measure that feeling on a scale of 1-10, with level 10 being the most intense, then to identify *where* in your body you feel the emotion. It is important to continue tapping on the feeling until you feel that the intensity has lowered significantly, preferably to a level 2-0 feeling in your body.

The Reframe Reclaim Round

At the end of every tapping script is what I call the *Reframe Reclaim Round*. A powerful way to recreate and *lock in* a new way of believing, thinking, acting, and manifesting.

I developed the process after using different versions of a number of modalities with clients, over time. The modalities include the work of Dr. Patricia Carrington, Dr. Joe Dispenza, Dr. Hew Lenn, Dr. Joe Vitale, and Professor Amy Cuddy.

I created the *Reframe Reclaim Round* for women in particular, based on the language that resonates most powerfully with our feminine wisdom – that reignites our passion, power, and purpose.

After working with hundreds of women, I began to see a pattern emerge. Most women I work with are incredibly intuitive and what I call *powerful dream weavers*. They know how to *manifest* what they want in their lives; it is just that over time that knowledge has been shattered. They don't need any more information; they simply need to find the key to access the deep feminine wisdom they already have!

So in order to find the key to your own inner wisdom and reignite your passion, power, and purpose – the *Reframe Reclaim Round* consists of a series of steps.

(Only after the intensity has dropped to a level 2-0, in the initial tapping script, should you move on to the *Reframe Reclaim Round* – not before! Otherwise, it's like putting a Band-Aid on a cut, without using a disinfectant first. It might look good for the moment, but it's not going to help that cut heal quickly.)

In the *Reframe Reclaim Round,* I will ask you create a detailed, clear picture of what you want to manifest in your life. To imagine you are your new self, right now, and that whatever intention you are creating is already manifest in your life. Then to create an accurate picture of your new reality, by asking a series questions. *Where are you? What's happening in this picture? How would you act differently, if this was already in your life? What words would you use? What actions would you take? Who would you spend time with? How would you choose to spend the moments in your day?*

Your *Higher Self,* through your intuition, will always provide you with just the right answers, when you have lowered the emotional intensity of the limiting beliefs of your past. The answers we need are always ready for us – it's just what we believe possible that stands in the way of hearing them!

Each of the *Reframe Reclaim Round* scripts then has four elements:

The first is *Choice*. Originally developed by Dr. Patricia Carrington in her work with EFT when she realized that for many people affirmations were a huge stretch (read more about why affirmations often don't work in Chapter 23).

For example, if you are in a job you hate and want to create a new job, perhaps you have been trying to say an affirmation like *I am now in my perfect job in the most perfect way.* But the truth of the matter is that you are not. That's the reality and continuing to say something that seems so far out of your grasp right now can feel overwhelming and daunting.

However, when you change that to say *I choose to believe it is possible to attract the most perfect job into my life,* the emphasis returns to your power. It's a proactive way to instill a new belief that you believe will eventually come to fruition − because you have chosen it!

In the *Reframe Reclaim Round*, we are powerfully stating what you now choose to believe, because first you have tapped to release the pattern that created the job you hated in the first place! Now *you* are deciding what *you* want to create! It's fun and a little bit exciting at the same time; starting with a blank slate and putting the power of choice right back in your own hands.

The second is *Gratitude.* Gratitude is a powerful way of creating success in your life and a practice I recommend to my clients to carry out daily. In the *Reframe Reclaim Round*, I add a statement of gratitude for your intention − even if it is yet to be there. Dr. Joe Dispenza's work in this field is outstanding. In his book *Breaking the Habit of Being Yourself,* he explains how gratitude increases your vibration and can change the way in which you live your life.

However, I also believe that we should have no attachment to the outcome of how the intention will play itself out. Rather, to practice gratitude, without the attachment to the outcome *you* are expecting; to be grateful for whatever way your intention will present itself.

The Universe has no time. That is a concept of our reality, and often we are limited by our own beliefs about how something will pan out. In most cases we have no idea of what we are truly capable of achieving. So to release our attachment to the outcome, but to expect a *better than I think possible* outcome, opens up the endless possibilities to create magic in your life!

This has certainly happened in my life. So many times I have intended something, and when I have gotten out of my own way, the outcome has been far greater than I believed possible. Only in hindsight have I truly understood this concept.

The experience of my life, as a parent of a child living with autism, reminds me of this constantly, and I find myself often saying, "If you had told me, 10 years ago, that this is how our life would be – I would never have believed it possible!"

Even though we intended the best possible outcome for our son, and our daughters, the reality is far greater than both Gerry and I could possibly have imagined. We just left that part up to the Universe and each of our *Higher Selves* to figure it out. I have to admit that their outcomes were pretty awesome and far greater than we could have imagined!

The third aspect is *Forgiveness*. In some of the tapping scripts, adding the element of forgiveness of yourself and of others is the way to free yourself from the confines of thoughts and emotions that simply do not serve you.

The practice of *Ho'oponopono* (pronounced ho-o-pono-pono) is an ancient Hawaiian practice of reconciliation and forgiveness, made famous by the work of Clinical Psychologist Dr. Ihaleakala Hew Len and bought to popularity by Dr. Joe Vitale in the book *Zero Limits*. The story of Dr. Hew Len and his healing of criminally insane inmates, without ever seeing or speaking with them, but simply through the practice of *Ho'oponopono*, is extraordinary; the story highlighting how the practice of forgiveness is a powerful way to release pain and suffering, within you! When we learn to forgive others and to forgive ourselves for whatever part we had to play in the outcome of an event, we are able to heal ourselves. Forgiveness is so powerful and one of the practices that can easily be incorporated into your life every single day.

Then finally at the end of the *Reframe Reclaim Round*, you will have the opportunity to powerfully lock in the new belief, using a *Power pose* with a powerful intention statement.

The *Power pose* is based on research by Social Psychologist and Harvard Professor Amy Cuddy, whose research about body language showed that assuming a *powerful pose* (think *Wonder Woman*, with hands on hips and legs planted firmly on the ground) can increase the hormone testosterone by as much as 20% and at the same time reduce the hormone cortisol by as much as 25%. (You can learn more about the pose from Amy's famous 2012 Ted Talk – *Your Body Language Shapes Who You Are.*)

What was interesting in her research was that this physiological change actually impacted biochemically, with 86% of *Power posers* reporting that they felt more likely to take chances, compared to those who stood in more passive poses (arms and legs crossed and a more slumped posture) where their testosterone levels dropped by 10% and cortisol levels rose by 15%!

Notwithstanding that posture and core strength are now huge issues for many women, as we sit more now than ever before, not only can the *Power pose* make you feel more powerful – but it can also impact on your posture – making you look more powerful (even if you are yet to feel it!).

Many clients have reported that adopting the *Power pose* alone, before an important meeting, has enabled them to stay focused and clear. In fact one of my clients reported that prior to a sales meeting with a previously difficult client she first tapped on her feelings of apprehension, and then adopted the *Power pose* in her mind. The sales meeting went better than she expected, with her client greeting her warmly and giving her an order that she had not expected.

There are many different versions of the *Reframe Reclaim Round*, dependent on the issue you are facing. In fact, when I am working with clients, there is actually no script to follow. It's very fluid, based on what the client tells me. But for the purposes of this book, I have used the scripts that I created to help my clients when they are tapping on their own and these can help get you started.

In the *Reclaim You Seminars* and programs (sallythibault.com. au/events) we are able to go into far more depth and intensity, including tapping to heal your younger self and projecting the image on your future self – all very powerful ways to create success in your life, but often difficult to do without a facilitator to guide you. I have experienced some powerful *Reframe Reclaim Rounds* not only for my clients, but also for myself, like re-setting a new way of thinking and a whole new way of manifesting what you want in your life. You just experience life differently!

A Word of Caution – And a Disclaimer

As you use some of the tapping scripts in the book, if you feel that you have triggered an event or memory that feels overwhelming, first just tap on the feelings of being overwhelmed (there is a tapping script for overwhelm in the bonus chapter), but then contact a qualified healthcare or EFT professional to help you.

Often times it is difficult to clear a block on your own. Tapping works by being as specific as you can, and sometimes that can be difficult. That's where a suitably qualified and certified EFT practitioner can help.

This book is not intended to replace medical care or treatment from a healthcare practitioner; rather, suggestions in the book are educational in nature and for your own self-improvement. So it is important that you take full responsibility for the following suggestions and scripts suggested in this book and if you feel you need support with overwhelming emotions or memories, that you seek the support of a qualified medical practitioner.

So are you ready? Let's reclaim the real you and reignite the passion, power, and purpose within!

CHAPTER 3

Creating a One-Word Theme

Just before the start of each New Year, I spend a few weeks deciding on a *One-word theme* for the next 12 months. After I have settled on a theme, I then begin the process of setting my intentions and plans for the year.

I have found this process so powerful because I'm a *bright shiny object* girl – *Oh! That looks good, I might try that!* Or – *Oh I haven't thought about that before – let's try that!* Choosing a *One-word theme* helps keep me focused on my intentions and plans.

While it is a great practice for the beginning of the year, it is also a powerful process to do at any time, to help keep you more focused.

Being focused is critical to manifesting success in your life, whether it is in your business or your personal life. We are always co-creating with our *Higher Self*. Whether you call that power *God, Source, Universe, The All That Is, The Dao* or *Tao* or whatever the word that most resonates with you. Your *Higher Self* has your best interests at heart and is co-creating with you – all the time!

But, and I emphasis a big *BUT* here, in order for your *Higher Self* to provide that support, you must adopt the belief that this is a 50/50 partnership. In other words, you must first decide what you want, then take the desired steps to put that intention in motion, staying focused, creating plans, setting intentions, and then *doing* what needs to be done. Your *Higher Self* will then assist you, often in the most extraordinary ways, showing up as opportunities, coincidences, gut feelings, or just plain luck!

Knowing what we want in the first place helps us manifest exactly what we want into our lives. But in the information overload world we live in, staying focused on *what we want* can be difficult.

I have found that the power of my *One-word theme* has helped enormously in both my personal life and in my business. It helps keep me on track in those moments of doubt, or if I find myself getting off track.

I began this process in 1997, the year my son was diagnosed with Asperger's Syndrome. The word I chose that year was *SOLUTIONS*.

After years of unknowing, and so much drama in our lives, I needed a year to sort out solutions to assist him in his life, and assist us in ours.

Surprisingly, at the end of that year, when I spent some time in review, I had indeed created *Solutions,* not only for our son but for our whole family.

It was the year I created what we now call the *School Report.* A document to help teachers and therapists understand my son and what we believed was important for him to achieve. It was later adopted within the school system and since then has been downloaded thousands of times from the *David's Gift* website.

During that *Solutions-themed* year, we also discovered a small school for him to transition to high school and found a fabulous social skills program for him to attend. We moved to a new home and attracted so many people who helped us to create solutions to so many challenges we had faced. I also created *The Art of Losing Weight Permanently* seminars – teaching and mentoring women to release the diet mentality and embrace intuitive eating. It was a *solution focused* year!

Since then I have chosen a different *One-word theme* each year. Some of the words have included *Peace, Abundance, Passion, Excellence, Focus, Success* and *Transform*, to name a few.

Over the years, the process has evolved. I wanted to make the word a powerful mantra. As a *bright shiny object* girl, I have a tendency to lose focus if things become boring, or allow fear to take over if I reach a stumbling block. So I decided to expand the *One-word theme* to create a series of questions from each of the letters that then expanded the theme even further, the questions creating a more powerful accountability structure to my intentions. As various opportunities arose throughout the year, or if I found myself falling into doubt or fear, I would simply refer to the theme and the questions. It always helps to realign my focus and get me back on track again.

Here's what I mean.

In 2014, I chose the word *SUCCESS*. From there, I took each of the letters and turned them into their own theme by creating questions or statements.

My word *SUCCESS* stood for a number of things:

S – *Self.* Does this allow me to express my true Self?

U – *Unwavering Focus.* How does this decision impact on my current intentions/goals? What level of Unwavering Focus is required to achieve success for me if I choose to do this?

C – *Commitment.* Can I be 100% Committed to this and how does it impact on the things already in my life?

C – *Captivating.* Is this Captivating for me? Is it a *Hell yes – I would LOVE to do this?*

E – *Excellence* in my EFT Practice. Does this move me one step closer to achieving Excellence in my field?

S – *Serendipity.* Does this feel Serendipitous? Is it in flow and does it resonate with my beliefs?

S – *Spiritual.* Does this allow me to embrace my true Spirit and Spirituality?

That was the year I started in a new role of as a women's mentor and EFT practitioner, and stepped away from my work in the field of autism. It was the year I also hired a business mentor and restructured my business. I also decided to redefine my friendship network and spend more time with like-minded people on the same path. In doing so, I made some powerful new connections with people who have since become good friends. By the end of the year, I had achieved exactly what I had set out to do at the beginning of the year.

My *One-word theme* was my powerful GPS system that kept me focused in times of doubt or fear.

My word for 2016 was *TRANSCENDENCE*, and finding that perfect word took a few weeks.

I wanted a word that encapsulated the intentions I want to achieve. After tapping almost daily for over three years, I know how powerful this modality is. I know and understand what happens at a deep cellular level when you clear limiting beliefs. So I wanted a word that would truly stretch what I believed possible for me. The dictionary meaning of *Transcendence* is – *'Going beyond ordinary limits; surpassing; exceeding. Existence or experience beyond the normal or physical level!'* Absolutely perfect!

So before I set any intentions, I do this process first. Work on it, think about it, question it, practice it, and tap on it. It does take a few weeks. I want to be truly comfortable with the word, and the statements, to ensure that they all resonate with what I want to achieve. Then when I feel really comfortable with the word, I begin the process of setting my 12-month, 90-day, and 30-day intentions, based on my *One-word theme*. But I do it a little differently than most.

Rather than creating 12-month goals, I prefer to create a vision for how I want my year to pan out. I have found over the past few years that 12-monthly goals or intentions just were not enough to keep me on track. Rather, creating 90-day and 30-day actionable intentions, with my *One-word theme* in mind, helps keeps me focused and strategic – and the whole process doesn't seem so daunting and overwhelming. Besides, I like to celebrate my successes along the way, and 12 months is just too long to wait for that special glass of champagne!

How to Create Your *One-Word Theme*

This is a tapping script with a bit of a difference and first there needs to be some background work. This process is so powerful it can actually change your life! So I encourage you to take time to choose your word. Because once you focus on this word, it will become a powerful guidepost and you may be very surprised at what will eventuate.

Try to set aside a couple of hours where you can be by yourself. I like to put on my favorite music, have some tea or some water handy, and set up in a place that makes me feel calm and serene, to allow my intuition to flow.

Next grab a dictionary, a large blank piece of paper, and some colored pens (I prefer to use gel pens or markers).

Then begin by asking yourself a series of questions and writing the answers on the paper.

What do you want to manifest in your life in the next 12 months? Some words to consider could be – *peace; tranquility; calm; abundance; clarity; direction; money; health; wisdom; freedom; partnerships; focus; success; empowerment; fulfillment; purpose.*

It is important just to let the words flow without editing. Just keep asking yourself the questions.

What is important for you to have in your life this coming year? What do you really want to embrace? How do you want this word to support you in your quest to rediscover your passion, power, and purpose?

Now look at the words you have written and see if any one word resonates with you. In the past, I have found that one in particular just seems to jump out at me, but sometimes there may be two or more.

Next, check the dictionary meaning of the word. Does the meaning resonate with what you want in your life? How does it feel when you say it? Does the meaning sum up what you would like to have or achieve?

Next ask yourself a further series of questions:

1. How does this word describe what I want to achieve for my health, my body, my relationships, my family, my career?
2. What would it mean for me if I choose this word?
3. What would have to change?
4. What would I have to start doing? What would I have to stop doing?

Once you feel that the word and the dictionary meaning have some resonance, it is time for the fun part.

Take each of the letters, and create a question or statement that fits with your theme – just as I did with my *SUCCESS* word.

After you have completed those steps, it's time to tap on any doubt or negative feelings you may be experiencing.

Tapping on Making Your *One-word Theme* Truly Powerful

First look at your word, then look at the statements and check how achievable they feel for you. Is there any doubt? Any fear? Or maybe memories where you set goals in the past, but not achieved them. Check to see how you feel about the past year. Was it a good year? Did you achieve what you wanted?

Next, try to *feel* where the emotion is in your body. Is it in your stomach? Your heart? Your head? Then measure the level of intensity on a scale of 1-10 (10 being the highest intensity) and write it down.

Let's start tapping:

Set-Up Statement: Even though I have this (intensity number) feeling as I am looking at this word, even though I want it to work I have this feeling that it won't, I deeply and completely accept myself and how I feel.

Set-Up Statement: Even though I have this (intensity number) feeling in my (where in your body) and I feel scared about committing to this word, what if it's wrong? I deeply and completely accept myself and how I feel.

Set-Up Statement: Even though I have this (emotion) feeling in my (where in your body) when I think about this word and what it could mean and I am worried I won't stick to it, I deeply and completely accept myself and how I feel.

EB: This (emotion) feeling.

SE: This feeling about this word.

UE: I really want this to be my theme, but I have failed in the past.

UN: This (emotion) feeling about creating goals or intentions that never work.

CHIN: This intense feeling of (emotion) for the times things like this haven't worked for me.

CB: This intense feeling of (emotion).

UA: I want this to work, but I just don't know.

Now, see if you can link any patterns or memories around times in the past when you have wanted something but it did not eventuate. (If not, just continue tapping on the feeling.)

Repeat one more time and then take a deep breath and measure the level of intensity in your body.

Once you are happy that the level of emotion has dropped to a 2-0 you can begin the Reframe Round.

Reframe Reclaim Round

Now imagine whatever you want to create is in your life right now. You are rewiring your beliefs, thoughts, and your actions to reflect what you want in your life. That includes acting as if it is already here!

Breathing in slowly and out slowly, create a picture in your mind of this reality and how it looks. How would you act differently, if this was already in your life? What words would you use? What actions would you take? Who would you spend time with? How would you choose to spend the moments in your day?

When you are ready, you can begin to tap.

Set-Up Statement: Even though I had this uncomfortable feeling, which is now a level (new level of intensity), I choose now to embrace this word as my theme for this next year. And I deeply and completely accept this new belief.

Set-Up Statement: Even though the uncomfortable feeling is no longer a strong feeling, I choose now to imagine what life would be like for me if I really followed this all year, and I deeply and completely accept this new belief in me.

Set-Up Statement: Even though I have released the intensity of times in the past when I haven't achieved what I wanted, I choose to be open to other limiting beliefs, and I choose to reclaim the beliefs that empower me and attract opportunities into my life in many ways. And I deeply and completely accept this new belief.

EB: I choose to allow myself to believe that this word could be possible in my life.

SE: I choose to release any and all self-imposed limiting beliefs about not getting what I want.

UE: I choose to allow ideas and opportunities that fit in with my theme to flow easily into my life.

UN: I choose to be open to all the possibilities that will now be part of my theme and my life.

CHIN: I choose to allow ideas and inspiration to flow.

CB: I am now grateful for all the new ideas and opportunities that are attracted to me in many ways.

UA: I am so grateful for the way in which this theme shows up in my life every day in many ways.

TH: I choose to embrace this way of being in all aspects of my life right now.

The Power Pose

Now stand with your hands on your hips, feet slightly apart (you can do this physically, or just imagine yourself doing it). Imagine that you are standing in the most powerful position you can. Your shoulders are back, your back is straight. You are lifting up from the core center of your body.

Create a powerful affirmation that resonates with you. (You can choose one of the statements in the script above or whatever statement *feels* right for you.)

Imagine that you are drawing up all the confidence, power, and knowledge you need through your feet and up into your heart. Then imagine that all that new energy and new affirmation is being distributed to every cell in your body. Keep breathing slow and deliberately. Hold this pose (or the image of this pose) for about 1 to 2 minutes, until you can feel this new energy powering in your body.

CHAPTER 4

Tapping to Create Powerful Intentions

After deciding on your *One-word theme*, the next step is to create the intentions you want to achieve, based on that theme.

To create what you want in your life, you have to first *state* what you want.

I have found in my experience working with clients that this is actually one of the biggest stumbling blocks. Most people can tell you what they *don't* want. But when asked what they *do* want, every single limiting, and often self-imposed, belief rises to the surface.

I have seen clients' hands shake and their heart race, and often they become quite agitated when I ask the question, "So, what do you want?"

Usually, they can paraphrase the answer really clearly, "Well I know what I don't want" – listing a whole range of things, often exactly the reality they live right now.

The co-creation partnership with our *Higher Self* goes on all the time. The problem is that we forget. We forget how powerful we really are. We forget that we have always co-created. Our body, our partner, our job, and the place we live, have all been co-created simply based on what we believe possible.

What stands in the way of creating a crystal clear vision of what we want is simply what we believe about ourselves. What we believe we are worthy of; what we believe we are capable of; our belief in ourselves and our willingness to trust in our own *Higher Self.*

But we first have to be crystal clear on what we want.

When you create that clarity, you begin the process of making your intentions a reality.

The only thing that will stand in the way of achieving your intentions is what you believe to be true for you. In this, and following chapters, you will discover how to release any limiting beliefs so that you stay in a constant state of clarity, co-creation, and flow.

So what is flow? I liken it to imagining you are in a stream of constant flowing energy. Like a flowing river, it just feels as if you are powerful, supported, and present. Like an unending flow of energy that you are able to access. Being *in flow* feels joyful, loving, and effortless. On the other hand, being *out of flow* feels frustrating, fearful, stressful, and hard.

Creating your *One-word theme*, and then backing that theme up with clear intentions, is the first step to creating that *flow* in your life.

All the way throughout this book you will see me use the word *intention,* rather than the word *goal.* The dictionary meaning of the word *intention* is '*what a person intends; a purpose or plan.*' The definition of the word *goal* is '*an objective.*' Our words are so powerful, so choosing what you want in your life starts by choosing words that best describe the energy you want. The word *intention* does just that!

So with your *One-word theme* in front of you, now is the time to *state* what you want to create, with some *kick-ass intentions* to make it a reality.

I also believe in setting small achievable intentions, broken down into 90-day and 30-day actionable intentions. A grand vision for what you want in your life is great, but that vision must also have a workable plan. A plan that keeps you motivated and inspired and where you can feel success helps keep you energized.

The reason is that things change. I have found that often times if you create an intention for a year or further, it is too easy to lose momentum and focus. There is nothing wrong with a long-term plan. But I have found that the 90-day and 30-day action plans allow you to tweak and readjust as you go. It feels more manageable and helps you stay much more focused and more powerful.

Taking the Whole of You With You!

The next part is to ensure that the *whole* of you and what is important in your world receives equal attention.

It serves no purpose to be successful in one area of your life – say your career – if your physical health suffers. The same applies for your faith or spiritual self. No amount of meditation will help you feel spiritual if you don't know where your next mortgage payment is coming from. And success won't feel very fulfilling if your relationship falls apart in the process.

So let's look at the four main areas of your life – or the four 'F's. Faith, Fitness, Family, Finance.

Faith – Represents your *Spiritual Self* – meditation, prayer, journaling, or tapping.

Fitness – Represents your *Physical world* – your mental fitness (reading or learning), physical fitness (exercise and nutrition), your environmental fitness (house, car, office).

Family – Includes the people who are important in your life – your key relationship, children, family, friends, co-workers, team, and clients.

Finance – Includes ways to enhance or improve your job or business, your finances and investments, or ways in which you can move to greater financial independence.

All four areas need to have the same amount of focus to truly create success.

So, first write down one or two things you would like to commit to in the next 90 days in those four areas.

- *Faith* could be – reading a spiritual book, journaling, meditating, tapping, or committing to writing what you are grateful for each day.
- *Fitness* could be – committing to a 90-day fitness plan, eating well, de-cluttering your home or office, deciding to read a self-help or motivational book.
- *Family* could be – choosing a date night once a week with your partner; playing a board game with your children; phoning a friend; setting aside time to ring/visit your parents; or sending a thank you card to at least one client a week.
- *Finance* could be – sorting out a budget, setting aside extra money to pay off your credit card, taking a workshop on marketing, or up-skilling or learning about investing.

When choosing intentions in any area, refer back to your *One-word theme* to ensure they fit with that framework of your theme. For *intentions* to really work, they require a six-step success strategy.

1. **Choice.** *I choose.* There is something very powerful in knowing that what you want to achieve is a choice!
2. **What.** *What* is the thing you really want to achieve? Be as specific as you can in this statement.

3. **Why.** Your *why* needs to have enough power to overcome the moments of doubt, procrastination, or fear.

4. **How.** The *how* is your course of action – your strategy. How will this fit into your day? What do you need to reschedule, change, put in or take out of your current schedule so that you have the time?

5. **Commitment.** What are you going to *commit* to doing each day to move you closer to your intention?

6. **Accountability.** What measures are you going to put into place to create accountability to the first five? Being accountable to somebody or something creates motivation. Setting up an accountability partnership is a great way to help you stay on track. Just a quick email, Facebook message, or phone call to your accountability partner, once a week, is a way to help you stay on track.

Next, take whatever you wrote down, and create one or two intentions you can focus on over the next 30 days.

Using the six-step Success Strategy, here are some examples:

Example of a Faith Intention

1. I choose to tap every day this month. (*Choice*)
2. To release that block I have about procrastination. (*What*)
3. So I can finish that project I have been working on, well before the deadline. (*Why*)
4. I will set aside 20 minutes a day. (*How*)
5. I will set my alarm to get up 20 minutes earlier each day. (*Commitment*)
6. I will write each of my tapping results in my journal. (*Accountability*)

Example of a Fitness Intention

1. I choose to lose the extra weight that makes me feel uncomfortable. *(Choice)*
2. I want to lose 2kg. *(What)*
3. So that I can fit into that fabulous dress I wore last winter, but is too tight for me this winter. *(Why)*
4. I will make daily healthier food choices to do this. *(How)*
5. I commit to making a green smoothie each day for breakfast. *(Commitment)*
6. I will keep a journal of what I eat every day. *(Accountability)*

Example of a Family Intention

1. I choose to spend more quality time with my husband. (*Choice*)
2. By planning a weekend away. (*What*)
3. So we can spend more time together, not always talking about the kids. (*Why*)
4. I will research places to go, and organize my mother to look after the kids. (*How*)
5. I will book the accommodation by the end of this week. (*Commitment*)
6. I will tell my husband the plan and ensure it's in both our diaries. (*Accountability*)

Example of a Finance Intention

1. I choose to pay make extra payments on my credit card. (*Choice*)
2. To pay off my credit card bill before the end of the month. (*What*)

3. The interest I save will go towards a holiday at the end of the year. (*Why*)
4. I will take my lunch and snacks to work. (*How*)
5. I commit to transferring an extra $100 per week into a savings account. (*Commitment*)
6. I will share this with my best friend so that she checks with me. (*Accountability*)

Whatever intention you choose to focus on, always refer to your *One-word theme* to see how your intentions fit with the theme you want. For example, say you chose the word *Success* – ask the questions, "How do these intentions fit with my theme? Do these intentions have an outcome that leads me in the direction I want? Does tapping each day fit into my success theme?" You get the idea!

As you write those things down, be very wary of any little voices in your head that are creating objections – remember those things we call *tail-enders*. The voice we try to ignore and pretend it's not there. But in the process of trying to ignore that voice, it becomes so powerful that it silently stops us from achieving.

As you are looking at each intention, be very aware of the thoughts that arise and the feelings that you feel in your body.

How does this intention make you feel? Scared, nervous, impossible, doubtful, *it's no use, nothing ever works for me anyway!* Whatever it is, write it down. Be truthful with yourself. The more honest you are, the more clarity you will discover. Those words are the very things that have held you back in the past, by pulling you out of flow.

The more *tail-enders* you can come up with, the more they help you uncover the patterns that are holding you back.

Even if the *tail-enders* feel silly or insignificant, write them down. Measure the intensity level from 1-10.

I also recommend that you journal regularly, each morning if possible, and especially when you tap. As I mentioned in an earlier chapter, once you have tapped and released the emotional intensity of any blocks that stand in your way, often you forget what the block was!

I have run into a number of clients who I have worked with in the past, and who have moved on to great things in their lives, but can't recall what we tapped on to release the block that was holding them back previously.

That is one of my favorite things about tapping; once you have released the limiting belief or block, it's gone! It's not as if you have to consciously change the way you think. When you release the belief you just begin to believe and act differently.

When you get into the habit of clearly stating what you want, it allows that wonderful manifestation process to begin. We are far more powerful than we give ourselves credit for. The clarity of our intention is just as important as the words that you use.

So for this exercise, just getting clear on what you want and writing it down begins the powerful process of making it a reality.

If you find it easy to decide what you want, skip to the next and subsequent chapters to find the specific tapping scripts to help you release limiting beliefs that may be sabotaging your success. But if you are still struggling to make the decision, Elizabeth's story may help.

Elizabeth's Story

Elizabeth had a dream to own her own business. She was 57, had four children, and she and her husband had been married for 35 years.

She had worked for a large department store in their homewares department for the last 20 years. Part-time at first, while her children were smaller, then as the children grew older and didn't need her as much at home, she gradually increased her hours.

But the hours were long. Her bosses often made her feel subordinate and powerless, and she had always had a dream of running her own business.

She had undertaken a few small business courses over the years, but she never felt confident enough to step out on her own. Besides, she didn't really know what it was that she wanted. She just felt that there was more to life than standing on her feet for eight hours a day working for somebody else.

Whenever she brought up the subject of running her own business, her husband wasn't very enthusiastic. They had a decent superannuation fund, some good savings, and they had paid off the mortgage on their house. As far as her husband was concerned, he didn't want to put their financial state in any jeopardy. Retirement was just around the corner and he had dreams of buying a caravan and travelling around Australia. (Elizabeth was not in the last bit excited about packing up the house, travelling for 12 months – and spending 24 hours a day with her husband!)

Elizabeth contacted me after being referred by a client from my eight-week program. She felt it would be the perfect thing for Elizabeth to do.

On our first call, I asked Elizabeth lots of questions about why she wanted to start a business. She talked a lot about being the boss, making her own decisions. Finally she said," I just feel that my life would have some value and purpose finally, but I just don't know what it is that I could do."

I asked her if there was a time in her life when she felt she was of no value.

"Oh, that's easy," she said, "most of my life."

So I asked her to tell me about her early years.

Elizabeth was the eldest of four children and the only girl. She had desperately wanted to go to university to study business. She was a bright student but also worked really hard at school to get good marks and was subsequently rewarded by gaining the entrance marks she needed. Her family lived in the country, so that also meant moving to live on campus. She was so excited, not only beginning the degree she wanted, but also living in the city.

However, during her first year, her mother became very ill and her father told Elizabeth she had to come home to help care for her. Even though her three brothers were all encouraged to go to school and get a degree, the same encouragement was not afforded to her. Her father told her that he felt it was best that she came home. He felt a degree was going to be a waste of time, as she would just end up getting married and having babies anyway!

So Elizabeth came home to their country property and cared for her mother until she passed away two years later.

By that stage, Elizabeth had met Roger, a local boy who worked at the service station in town as a mechanic. They married not long after. She and Roger moved a number of times throughout those years as Roger built his car repair business. It seemed with each subsequent baby, another opportunity arose and a move happened not long after. Elizabeth enjoyed being a stay at home mother and supporting Roger in his business. But she felt there was always something missing in her life.

Twenty years ago, they bought a franchised car servicing business, and moved to the city. One Christmas, Elizabeth took a job in a department store to help with the family finances. After the Christmas season was over, she was asked by management to stay on.

When I asked her what she wanted, tears welled up in her eyes and she said, "I honestly don't know. It seemed that whenever I wanted something I couldn't have it. It was taken from me, or there was a reason I couldn't complete it. It is as if in my whole life, other people's needs are more important than mine."

So I asked Elizabeth to first write down what she wanted from having her own business:

1. To feel I am in control of my destiny.
2. To feel valued.
3. To do what I want to do, without feeling that others' needs are more important.

I asked her first how each of those statements made her feel. She said each represented something she wanted to feel in her life.

So we took each statement one at a time. I asked her when she first felt she had no control of her destiny, and immediately she said, "When my Dad told me to come home from university."

I asked her to try to recall how that felt and she said, "It was like I had no value, that others' needs were more important to mine. I believed that by studying business I could control my own destiny, feel that I was valued, and could contribute to our family."

At that moment, she stopped and said, "Everything I want in a business now!"

So we tapped on each of those feelings. Finally, she said, "You know, this is all about my Dad. I wanted to do something, I didn't know what, just to show him that I was worth more than just looking after kids. Oh for heaven's sake, I can't make a decision because I am trying to please my Dad – not please me!"

Tapping for When You Don't Know What You Want

As in Elizabeth's case, if you are having trouble deciding what you want, write down what you want to *feel* and *why*.

If it is a relationship you want to attract, write down *why* you want a relationship and what type of person you would like to attract.

If you want to lose weight, write down the *why*. What do you want to achieve or feel if you lose the weight?

Now measure the *feeling* in your body when you ask the question, "What do I really want?"

Is it confusion? Is it frustration? Is it fear? Is it sadness? Is it a sense of *what's the point?*

Next, try to *feel* where the emotion is in your body. Is it in your stomach, your heart, or your head? Then measure the level of intensity on a scale of 1-10 (10 being the highest intensity) and write it down.

Let's start tapping:

Set-Up Statement: Even though I have this (intensity number) feeling because I am not sure what I want, I deeply and completely accept myself and how I feel.

Set-Up Statement: Even though I have this (intensity number) feeling in my (where in your body) about not knowing what I really want, and it makes me feel (emotion), I deeply and completely accept myself and how I feel.

Set-Up Statement: Even though I have this (emotion) feeling in my (where in your body) whenever I think about what I want, and I just don't know, I deeply and completely accept myself and how I feel.

EB: This (emotion) feeling.

SE: This uncomfortable feeling.

UE: I didn't realize that this feeling ran so deep.

UN: This (emotion) feeling of not knowing what I want.

CHIN: This intense feeling of (emotion) because I am not sure what I want.

CB: This intense feeling of (emotion).

UA: I just am not sure what I want.

TH: This overwhelming feeling I just don't know what I really want.

See if you can link any patterns or memories around never getting what you want, or deciding what you want. (If not, just continue tapping on the feeling.)

Repeat one more time and then take a deep breath and measure the level of intensity in your body.

Once you are happy that the level of emotion has dropped to a 2-0 you can begin the Reframe Round.

Reframe Reclaim Round

Now imagine whatever you want to create is in your life right now. You are rewiring your beliefs, thoughts, and your actions to reflect what you want in your life. That includes acting as if it is already here!

Breathing in slowly and out slowly, see if you can create a picture in your mind of this reality and how it looks. How would you act differently, if this was already in your life? What words would you use? What actions would you take? Who would you spend time with? How would you choose to spend the moments in your day?

When you are ready, you can begin to tap.

Set-Up Statement: Even though I had this uncomfortable feeling, which is now a level (new level of intensity), I choose now to be comfortable and confident in allowing what I want to be presented to me. And I deeply and completely accept this new belief.

Set-Up Statement: Even though the uncomfortable feeling is no longer a strong feeling, I choose now to imagine what life would be like if I knew what I really wanted, and I deeply and completely accept this new belief in me.

Set-Up Statement: Even though I have released the intensity of not knowing what I want, I choose to be open to other limiting beliefs, and I choose to reclaim the beliefs that empower me and attract opportunities into my life in many ways. And I deeply and completely accept this new belief.

EB: I choose to allow myself time to discover what I really want.

SE: I choose to release any and all self-imposed limiting beliefs about what I really want.

UE: I choose to allow ideas and opportunities to flow easily into my life.

UN: I choose to be open to all the possibilities that could be the perfect thing for me to do.

CHIN: I choose to allow ideas and inspiration to flow.

CB: I am now grateful for all the new ideas and opportunities that are attracted to me in many ways.

UA: I am so grateful for the knowledge that shows up in my life every day in many ways.

TH: I choose to embrace this way of being in all aspects of my life right now.

The Power Pose

Now stand with your hands on your hips, feet slightly apart (you can do this physically, or just imagine yourself doing it). Imagine that you are standing in the most powerful position you can. Your shoulders are back, your back is straight. You are lifting up from the core center of your body.

Create a powerful affirmation that resonates with you. (You can choose one of the statements in the script above or whatever statement *feels* right for you.)

Imagine that you are drawing up all the confidence, power, and knowledge you need through your feet and up into your heart. Then imagine that all that new energy and new affirmation is being distributed to every cell in your body. Keep breathing slow and deliberately. Hold this pose (or the image of this pose) for about 1 to 2 minutes, until you can feel this new energy powering in your body.

CHAPTER 5

Tapping on Being Comfortable to Ask for What You Want

This chapter is about releasing any limiting beliefs or discomfort around asking for what you want, and having what you want.

This was the case with my client, Debbie.

Debbie joined the *Tapping to Reclaim You* program because she was feeling unhappy with her life. From the outside, she had the ideal life. She was happily married to her husband for over 25 years (or at least to others it seemed happy) and together they had two teenage boys. Her husband had his own business which had given them both, together with her job, an enviable lifestyle.

But lately, her relationship with her husband had become tenuous. They often argued over insignificant things that quickly escalated to shouting matches, leading to days where they didn't communicate with each other.

She had gained 10 kilos in the last year, which made her feel uncomfortable and tired all the time. She was beginning to resent her job, her children, and often her husband. She just felt stuck and frustrated with life.

She had worked hard to reach management level at her company, working up from an intern to managing a staff of 60 people. Although she loved her job she felt she always had to work harder than anybody else in the same position. While she prided herself on taking on difficult challenges, it annoyed her that others seemed to gain rewards but did far less work than she did.

Consequently, she was anxious and short tempered most of the time. Her husband's patience was wearing thin, as he kept saying to her, "What else do you want? I don't know what to do to make you happy."

Debbie knew it was not up to her husband to make her happy, and that made it all the harder for her. She was well respected, earned good money, and liked the people she worked with. But she found herself feeling flat and low in energy most days.

When she got home at night she would find fault with her boys. She found herself yelling at them most nights to clean their rooms or get off the computer. She would become even more infuriated when they would roll their eyes and say things like, "What now, Mum?" She hated that she seemed to yell at them all the time, but she couldn't seem to control her anger and frustration.

When Debbie first came onto the program, I could feel the envy the other participants had for her. And the questioning that was going on in their minds. *What the heck is she doing here?* (Part of being an experienced EFT practitioner is learning to read people's faces!) She is very attractive, intelligent, and funny, with an energy that precedes her as she walks into a room.

It wasn't until the middle of the second day of the program that we got to the cause of Debbie's frustrations.

One of the processes of the weekend was to bring a food along to the event that you want to tap on to release any emotional intensity. The reasons behind these cravings are always as surprising as the food craving itself!

Debbie bought chocolate éclairs.

"This is my 'go to' food," said Debbie. "Whenever I am stressed or frustrated, I just reach for these. I have a favorite French Patisserie near my home, and they know me by name. As soon as they see my car they are boxing up six éclairs! I tell them they are for my husband and boys ... but they often don't make it out of the car!"

As we began the process, I asked her to explain what the éclair reminded her of. She told me that her grandmother was French and used to make chocolate éclairs often. It was Debbie's favorite thing to do.

She loved sitting in the kitchen while her grandmother rolled out the pastry. She loved the smell of the kitchen while they were baking, and then waiting for them to cool. She would often help her grandmother fill the pastry with cream and cover the top with melted chocolate. But the part she loved most was to sit with her grandmother and eat the éclairs and drink hot sweet tea with her.

I asked her how that memory made her feel now as she retold the story. She said, "I felt safe. Like no matter what was happening in the world, making and eating éclairs with my grandmother made me feel really, really safe."

We started tapping on the taste of the éclairs and the feelings of being safe. "Even though I taste the sensation of the chocolate and it feels warm and safe, I deeply and completely accept myself," and continued on the round.

Debbie began to cry uncontrollably, as we continued tapping. I asked her to look at me while we continued tapping.

As the emotion started to subside, I asked her to continue tapping while sharing her story.

When she was a little girl, her mother and father used to work long hours so she would go to her grandparents' house every afternoon after school. Her grandparents' house was not far from her school and she had to walk back to their home in the afternoons by herself. She remembered a feeling of being frightened when she walked home, but couldn't recall what it was.

We continued to tap on feeling frightened. A memory flashed into her mind of one afternoon walking home by herself. She recalled having to walk past some older boys from the high school that was adjacent to the primary school she attended. The boys were all standing outside of a house in her street.

As she walked past, one of the bigger boys grabbed her school bag from her back and threw it into the front yard of the house. No matter how many times she pleaded with them, they would not let her get the bag.

I asked her to recall how she got the bag. She said, "I couldn't do it myself. No matter how hard I tried. I don't recall how it ended up on my back, but I remember running home as fast as I could. I didn't tell my grandmother what happened. I think I remember one of the boys yelling at me, 'Don't be a cry-baby, cry-babies don't get what they want,' – or something like that."

When she got home, the chocolate éclairs were on the table, and she remembered eating one so she wouldn't cry!

I asked Debbie if she could recall other times in her life when she felt that she had to work hard to get things. She began to talk about times in her life where she just felt that she worked harder than anybody else to get the same level of success.

The more we tapped the more she remembered, and then suddenly she said, "Every time I feel stressed or way out of my comfort zone I reach for éclairs. Every time I feel overwhelmed like I have to do this all by myself, the éclairs just make me feel better, it's that safe feeling. Every time I get cranky with my husband and my sons, because I feel I have to do everything myself, I reach for the éclairs!"

After we had finished a round of tapping, I asked her to take another bite of the éclair. She said, "This actually makes me feel quite ill, just to look at it!" She threw the éclair into the garbage.

When her emotional intensity was down, we then created a reframe round. "Even though, in the past, I believed it was hard and unsafe to get what I want, I choose now to believe that everything I want comes to me easily and effortlessly."

A few weeks later Debbie messaged me to say that her energy levels were higher than they had ever been. She was feeling much more focused in her work and she and her husband were planning a trip away together – and she had not had a craving for a chocolate éclair since!

I mentor many women who feel uncomfortable to both ask for what they want and have what they want, whether it is a product of the time we grew up in, or a product of our family's belief system. Or in Debbie's case, an event from her childhood that triggered a memory that everything was hard to get. That memory created a belief that played out as a pattern in her life.

Whenever you create an intention and it creates a feeling or a stress around the words – there is something that needs to release. Our feelings hold the key. If you have a negative or uncomfortable feeling around asking for what you want – don't ignore it; instead, question it. *What makes me feel uncomfortable about this intention? Why do I have this hesitancy? What is the fear I feel? Why do I have trouble asking for what I want?*

Our feelings hold the solution and the key. The problem is that often we have been taught to ignore the emotion or feeling. But there are two issues with that:

1. You don't believe that you are capable of creating what you want in your life.
2. Even if you do achieve success, it may be short lived because you may have a belief that you don't deserve to have what you want.

It's one of the reasons why people lose weight and then put it back on again. They create a goal to lose weight, think it is all about the food and exercise, so go on a strict diet or exercise program for 8 or 12 weeks. Then it all gets too hard because the underlying feelings and emotions haven't been dealt with. So they return to old habits – and the weight piles back on again (usually more!).

Those feelings are often so intense they keep us trapped in a cycle where the core belief is far stronger than any intention.

So in today's tapping go back and look at what you have intended and then check in on the feelings you get when you state the intention out loud. Are there any feelings of hesitancy around asking for, or getting, what you want? Are there memories of not getting what you wanted in the past, or never feeling as if you had a right to ask for what you wanted?

Tapping on Being Comfortable to Ask for What You Want

As you read the intention out loud, measure the level of emotion around feeling that it is okay for you to ask and get what you want.

Try to *feel* where the emotion is in your body, and what level of intensity you believe it to be true. Write down both.

Let's start tapping:
Set-Up Statement: Even though I have this uncomfortable feeling in asking for what I want, I deeply and completely accept myself and how I feel.

Set-Up Statement: Even though I have this (intensity number) feeling in my (where in your body) about not feeling comfortable in asking for what I want and it makes me feel (emotion), I deeply and completely accept myself and how I feel.

Set-Up Statement: Even though I have this (emotion) feeling in my (where in your body) whenever I think about asking for and getting what I want easily, I deeply and completely accept myself and how I feel.

EB: I feel (emotion) when I think about asking for what I want.
SE: This (emotion).
UE: I find it really hard to ask for what I want.
UN: This (emotion).
CHIN: This feeling of being uncomfortable in asking for what I want that makes me feel (emotion).
CB: This (emotion).
UA: This (emotion) feeling.
TH: This overwhelming discomfort in asking for what I want.

See if you can link any patterns or memories around never getting what you want, or making a decision about what you want. (If not, just continue tapping on the feeling.)

Repeat one more time and then take a deep breath and measure the level of intensity in your body.

Once you are happy that the level of emotion has dropped to a 2-0 you can begin the Reframe Round.

Reframe Reclaim Round

Now imagine as if whatever you want to create is in your life right now. You are rewiring your beliefs, thoughts, and your actions to reflect what you want in your life. That includes acting as if it is already here!

Breathing in slowly and out slowly, see if you can create a picture in your mind of this reality and how it looks. How would you act differently, if this was already in your life? What words would you use? What actions would you take? Who would you spend time with? How would you choose to spend the moments in your day?

When you are ready, you can begin to tap.

Set-Up Statement: Even though I had this uncomfortable feeling, which is now (intensity number), I choose now be comfortable and confident in asking for what I want. And I deeply and completely accept this new belief.

Set-Up Statement: Even though the uncomfortable (emotion) is no longer a strong feeling, I choose now to imagine what life would be like if I felt confident in asking for what I want all the time. And I deeply and completely accept this new belief in me.

Set-Up Statement: Even though I feel I have released this uncomfortable feeling in asking for what I want, I choose to be open to other limiting beliefs, and I choose to reclaim the beliefs that empower me and attract opportunities into my life in many ways. And I deeply and completely accept this new belief.

EB: I choose to allow myself to embrace this new confident feeling.

SE: I choose to release any and all self-imposed limiting beliefs about my confidence in asking for what I want.

UE: I choose to allow confidence in asking for what I want to flow easily into my life.

UN: I choose to be open to all the possibilities that would allow confidence in asking for what I want to flow into my life.

CHIN: I choose to embrace this new confident feeling.

CB: I am now grateful for this new confidence in asking for and receiving what I want and the way in which opportunities are attracted to me in many ways.

UA: I am so grateful for the confidence that shows up in my life every day in many ways.

TH: I choose to embrace this new confidence in all aspect of my life.

The Power Pose

Now stand with your hands on your hips, feet slightly apart (you can do this physically, or just imagine yourself doing it). Imagine that you are standing in the most powerful position you can. Your shoulders are back, your back is straight. You are lifting up from the core center of your body.

Create a powerful affirmation that resonates with you. (You can choose one of the statements in the script above or whatever statement *feels* right for you.)

Imagine that you are drawing up all the confidence, power, and knowledge you need through your feet and up into your heart. Then imagine that all that new energy and new affirmation is being distributed to every cell in your body. Keep breathing slow and deliberately. Hold this pose (or the image of this pose) for about 1 to 2 minutes, until you can feel this new energy powering in your body.

CHAPTER 6

Tapping on Believing it's Possible

In his book *Breaking the Habit of Being Yourself*, Dr. Joe Dispenza says, *"We talk ourselves out of our own genius."*

I remember the day I read that quote. I read it twice, highlighted it and wrote it down, and it forms one of the sessions in the *Reclaim You* seminars.

They are such a powerful set of eight words and they have been the key to releasing a number of self-imposed limitations in my own life.

I can recall so many times when I would create an intention and opportunities would appear. But then I simply *talked myself out of them*. I made excuses, or I procrastinated or justified the opportunities as not being the right ones. I would then simply tell myself that whatever I wanted wasn't right; or that if it was meant to be it would have been; or a myriad of other excuses. Those excuses simply wrapped around a belief that I wasn't good enough to have what I wanted!

While I was very committed to creating some rather big intentions for myself, the fact was I didn't believe in myself enough to make them a possibility. The loudest words in my brain were the words: *You can't do that! Who you think you are?*

It was a core belief I carried most of my life – I simply talked myself out of my own genius, all the freaking time!

I often hear people say, "I am leaving it up to the Universe", or "It's now out of my hands and up to the Universe". My next question is always, "Do you really want this?" and then "Do you believe that you have done enough to make this a reality?"

In his book *Secrets of a Millionaire Mindset*, author T. Harv Ecker says, "I have yet to meet a person meditating under a tree and a bag of money falls on his head!"

So it is true for anything we want in life; co-creating is a 50/50 game. Your job is to be very clear on what you want, create clear intention, then a plan and keep moving. Then to be open and ready for the opportunities that your *Higher Self* will present to you. As Oprah Winfrey once said, "Luck is preparation meeting opportunity."

The problem is that often times we are looking for the bag of gold to drop on our heads. The miracle, the sure thing, the guarantee, instead of the tiny little opportunities, coincidences, or feelings that remind you that you are right on track – or even if you need to make a few adjustments to the original intention! We forget that we are powerful co-creators in making our intentions a reality, and while the opportunities are all around us, we talk ourselves out of them because they do not look like the bag of gold!

It's a process often referred to as *Frequency of Illusion* and *Confirmation Bias*.

The *Frequency of Illusion* works like this: Have you ever decided that you really liked and wanted a particular type of car? Let's say a black BMW.

The very minute you decide you want that black BMW you see them everywhere, right? On the highway next to you; in the shopping center car park; outside your office.

This is because our brains begin to filter out all the extraneous stuff around us to enable us to focus on what we have attuned to. There is simply too much going on in our world for us to be aware of everything in our vision or awareness.

As I am writing this book at the moment, there is a new housing development being constructed across the road from our house. Some days, the noise and the vibration of the construction machinery just drive me crazy! On other days, like today, I hardly notice. Why? It simply comes down to what I choose to focus on.

Right now, I am focusing intently on the writing, so it's like my other senses filter out the noise. It is only now that I choose to focus on the noise that I can actually hear the machines. Ten minutes ago I didn't even notice the noise.

As a further example, psychologists at the University of Utah conducted an experiment, where they filmed a group of students playing with basketballs. Viewers were asked to count the number of times the students passed the ball to each other. While the video is playing, a person in a gorilla suit walks through the middle of the players. Incredibly, the scientists discovered that of the people who watched the video and could count how many times the ball was passed, as many as 40% of them failed to see the gorilla.

That is *Frequency of Illusion* – our ability focus almost exclusively on what we want to focus on, filtering out things that are not important to us.

The second part of that is called *Confirmation Bias*. This is where our brain constantly seeks to reaffirm what we believe, again, attuning your focus to what you believe to be true about yourself and about life.

If you believe that the world is a scary place, your focus will shift to seeing things that constantly reaffirm that belief.

(Insurance companies are masters at honing in on our greatest fears – to make us buy insurance!)

The opposite, however, is also true. If you believe that the world is a kind and generous place, then you will notice kindness and generosity everywhere, reaffirming what you believe to be true.

But let's take the example of the BMW again. You would really love to own a black BMW, so you see them everywhere (*Frequency of Illusion*). However, deep down you don't really believe that you could ever afford a BMW.

All of a sudden you find yourself in all sorts of situations where your belief about your inability to own a BMW will be validated.

You will be at a party and somebody will start talking about the problems he has had with his BMW. You will read an article about how expensive BMW mechanical repairs are. You will be at a family BBQ and your uncle will tell you about the guy who ripped him off who drove a black BMW.

Your awareness is tuned to those messages confirming your underlying belief about your ability to afford or own a car like a BMW (*Confirmation Bias*).

So it is true in life.

In order to create what you want in life, first you must be crystal clear on what you do want. Then be mindful of what happens next because:

> Our beliefs determine our thoughts.
> Our thoughts become our emotions.
> Our emotions turn into our feelings.
> Our feelings determine our words.
> Our words influence our actions.
> And our actions become our reality.

If you want to change the last – you need to change the first.

In order to change your reality, you first have to change what you *believe* possible and what you *believe* you are worthy of manifesting in your life.

No amount of intention setting, words, or actions will create lasting success – if your beliefs about what you *believe* possible are incongruent.

It is the beliefs *you* have about *you* that hold the key to your success.

When I first started tapping, stating the truth of how I was feeling was often the most uncomfortable part of the whole process. It felt so foreign. I didn't want to say the negative things, in case they came true! But the more I tapped the more I realized that in the past instead of acknowledging that negative belief, I just pretended it wasn't there. The problem was, the patterns kept repeating themselves – over and over again! The same ones!

So while I wanted to create change and success in my life, there were many events from my past that locked in the belief that I wasn't smart enough, clever enough, or worthy enough to have success in my life. So many times I would find myself on the brink of being successful and I would end up walking away or sabotaging it. Simply because my core beliefs didn't match what I believed possible.

My Story

I tap every day and have done so for the last three years. But there was one pattern I couldn't seem to clear. I didn't believe that I could create success in doing what I was really passionate about. There was a part of me that was always hanging on to *having another option*, a Plan B! That if I didn't succeed at this, then I could always go back to working in marketing, or customer service.

I didn't realize that holding on to my '*I have another option*' belief was holding me back from taking my business to the level of success I wanted.

So one month, I decided to make the word *Success* my tapping theme for the month. I often undertake 30-day themes as a way to keep me accountable to my tapping.

There was one story that kept coming up in my tapping that was linked to this feeling of not feeling safe around success. I had tapped around it for ages, but couldn't seem to shift the feeling about not being safe. One morning I tapped on an incident that was pivotal in releasing the fear of not being safe and the limiting belief of *the other option!* It is amazing how freeing and energizing it is to finally acknowledge the fact that you have nothing else to fall back on. Your focus and commitment changes very quickly!

In the past, every time I would think about setting *out of my comfort zone* intentions, I would immediately feel fear or foreboding. I just thought it was because it was out of my comfort zone, but it was always there.

I tapped on it many times, but I couldn't quite get the feeling down to a 2 or a 0.

I have always been great at creating intentions; sometimes setting intentions that were absolutely impossible to achieve in the time I had set myself. You see, I had an underlying belief that even though success was possible for others, it was not possible for me. To validate that belief I set impossible intentions just to prove I was right!

So one morning, while tapping on my *Success* theme, I could feel the fear rise again. I had a speaking event coming up but every time I went to start work on my presentation, I had this weird feeling of dread come over me.

On this particular morning, while tapping on fear of success, I started to recall a memory from my school years. I had always been a good student in my junior school years, in the top 10% and often the top of a subject. However, in high school I struggled. In fact with each subsequent year, I fell behind more and more. When I reached Year 11, it became very obvious that I was not going to pass my final year, unless something changed dramatically.

I had my heart set on studying to be a teacher. As long as I could remember, that's all I wanted to do. So during the last term of Year 11, my parents came to a meeting with the Head of Year. The meeting was to discuss subject choices for Year 12, based on what I wanted to do after I left school.

At the meeting, the Head of Year asked what I wanted to do after school, and I said confidently, "I want to go to Teachers College; I really want to be a teacher."

I remember the look on her face when she turned to me and said, "Sally, let's be honest dear, you are really not clever enough to be a teacher. We need to look at other options for you."

Fast-forward 40 years and when that memory came up for me while I was tapping, the intensity of the emotion went straight up to about a level 9! (I am always amazed at this process of tapping! Just when I think I have cleared something, another one unfolds, often taking me by surprise. This was one of those!)

Being a teacher was the only passion I had. It was all I ever wanted to do. I remember the crushing feeling in the pit of my stomach. *But that's what I am here to do and if I can't do that – what else can't I do?*

I could see my 15-year-old self, sitting in that chair, feeling so confused. When I was little, my favorite thing to do was to coerce my three sisters and brother to play, pretending to be at school while we were on holidays. I would spend hours creating work plans and activities – just like teachers did.

In my mind, while I was tapping, I could feel the incredible sadness of my 15-year-old self with all those crushed dreams. The only thing I wanted to do was suddenly taken away.

If I couldn't do that – what else was not possible in my life?

From that moment I could see how the pattern of my life had played out. I believed what that Head of Year told me about not being smart enough to be a teacher, and I failed Year 12. I went on to go to a business college, which I hated. I got jobs in offices, which again I hated. Then when I found what I wanted to do – which at first was teaching aerobics – I loved it, but eventually sabotaged my success before anybody else could take it away from me. That then created another pattern for me where I would become successful at something then walk away. It was safer to walk away from success, to *other options*, before somebody took my dream away!

As the awareness opened up, suddenly so many patterns of my life began to make sense. At the same time, I suddenly recognized the *other option* pattern. It was the pattern I had created. When life got too hard, when success became too scary, when nobody around me believed in me – I could always opt out and get a job! There it was, right there. It was one of those moments where I was just so grateful for this incredible technique. It was then I made a decision that there was no *other option,* this was finally it! (It's pretty cool when you get those realizations in your 50s.)

The patterns of our lives are *not us* – we are perfect.

We are unique and wonderful and able to do and achieve anything we want. And when we are stuck – it's just a pattern. It's just a pattern that can be cleared and healed so that we can get back on track again.

The challenge we face is to not fall into the limiting belief. But rather be mindful of our thoughts, our emotions, our feelings, our words, and our actions. Because they hold the clue to the pattern that stops us from being all we can be.

When you find the cause of the pattern you can release it and recreate a new one, with new outcomes! It's just that simple.

Tapping on Believing it's Possible

For this exercise, go back and look at the intention you wrote in Chapter 4.

As you read the intention out loud, measure the level of emotion around believing that this intention is possible.

Try to *feel* where the emotion is in your body, and what level of intensity you believe it to be true. Write down both.

Let's start tapping:

Set-Up Statement: Even though I have this doubt that my intention is possible, I deeply and completely accept myself and how I feel.

Set-Up Statement: Even though I have this (level of intensity) belief about not believing that this intention will manifest in my life and it makes me feel (emotion), I deeply and completely accept myself and how I feel.

Set-Up Statement: Even though when I think about this doubt, and I can recall other times when I have not achieved what I wanted to and I feel this emotion in my (where in your body), I deeply and completely accept myself and how I feel.

EB: This doubt.
SE: I have this doubt that I can make this happen.
UE: This high level of doubt.
UN: I have done this before.
CHIN: This doubt sometimes overwhelms me.

CB: Maybe it's not possible after all.

UA: This overwhelming doubt.

TH: This doubt that I can achieve this intention.

Repeat one more time and then take a deep breath and measure the level of intensity in your body.

See if you can link any patterns or memories around not achieving something you wanted in your past.

Once you are happy that the level of emotion has dropped to a 2-0 you can begin the Reframe Round.

Reframe Reclaim Round

Now imagine whatever you want to create is in your life right now. You are rewiring your beliefs, thoughts, and your actions to reflect what you want in your life. That includes acting as if it is already here!

Breathing in slowly and out slowly, see if you can create a picture in your mind of this reality and how it looks. How would you act differently, if this was already in your life? What words would you use? What actions would you take? Who would you spend time with? How would you choose to spend the moments in your day?

When you are ready, you can begin to tap.

Set-Up Statement: Even though I had this doubt, which is now a (level of intensity), I choose now to be comfortable and confident in believing this is possible in my life. And I deeply and completely accept this new belief.

Set-Up Statement: Even though the doubt is no longer a strong feeling, I choose now to imagine what life would be like if I truly believed I could achieve this. And I deeply and completely accept this new belief in me.

Set-Up Statement: Even though I feel I have released this feeling of doubt, I choose to be open to other limiting beliefs, and I choose to reclaim the beliefs that empower me and attract opportunities into my life in many ways. And I deeply and completely accept this new belief.

EB: I choose to allow myself to believe it is possible to achieve this intention.

SE: I choose to release any and all self-imposed limiting beliefs about my ability to achieve this intention.

UE: I choose to allow my belief in the possibility to flow easily into my life.

UN: I choose to be open to all the possibilities that would allow this intention to flow into my life.

CHIN: I choose to believe this is possible for me to achieve.

CB: I am now grateful for this new belief, and the way in which opportunities are attracted to me in many ways.

UA: I am so grateful for many ways the opportunities continue to show up in my life every day in many ways.

TH: I choose to believe that I will achieve this intention right now.

The Power Pose

Now stand with your hands on your hips, feet slightly apart (you can do this physically, or just imagine yourself doing it). Imagine that you are standing in the most powerful position you can. Your shoulders are back, your back is straight. You are lifting up from the core center of your body.

Create a powerful affirmation that resonates with you. You can choose one of the statements in the script above or whatever statement *feels* right for you.

Imagine that you are drawing up all the confidence, power, and knowledge you need through your feet and up into your heart. Then imagine that all that new energy and new affirmation is being distributed to every cell in your body. Keep breathing slow and deliberately. Hold this pose (or the image of this pose) for about 1 to 2 minutes, until you can feel this new energy powering in your body.

CHAPTER 7

Tapping to Release the Power of Words

When working with clients I am literally hanging on every word they say; I listen intently, and without judgment, waiting for a pattern to evolve.

Our words give us away all the time. They reflect what we believe, often without us being really aware of just how powerful they are.

I love just allowing my clients to talk and tell their story and as they do, I am listening for the thread that is holding the belief together. Their words often hold the secret key to some very powerful yet tragic stories. The most powerful of those stories are from survivors of sexual abuse or domestic violence.

When I first started out in my EFT mentoring, I thought that it was odd that I seemed to attract women who had experienced abuse in their lives. I thought perhaps it was just a coincidence. I have come to learn that it is more common than I thought.

Many times, I sit in quiet admiration for these women who, for most of their lives, have hidden such incredibly painful secrets;

the ramifications of the abuse impacting on their lives in many ways. But the other side of the story was often that when they reached out for help from others, they were not believed. The feelings of unworthiness, pain, and sadness were intensified by their cry for help being ignored.

I am so grateful for the power of this amazing modality of tapping. Not only can it help release and heal the pain of years of abuse, it can allow them to create lives far greater than they believed possible.

I have heard some painfully sad stories in my time as an EFT practitioner and professional counselor, but Judy's story still stays with me today.

Judy's Story

Judy came to see me after a recommendation from a friend.

She had been suffering from fibromyalgia for years, and was prescribed numerous medications, including anti-depressants, which she felt caused her to gain weight. While she experienced some relief from the pain, she felt the anti-depressants made her feel as if she was disconnected from the world.

She contacted me after a friend told her about tapping and food cravings.

While Judy ate a relatively healthy diet, she noticed that when she ate certain foods the pain seemed to flare up, and bread seemed to be the trigger food for her. She had tried numerous times to give up eating bread, and she had managed to keep her symptoms at bay. But invariably, as soon as she felt a little better, she would find herself reaching for bread again, without being consciously aware of it, until the pain flared up again.

Judy was 75 years old.

As we started tapping on the food craving I asked her to first describe the sensation of smelling the bread. She said, "The smell of the bread is soothing and calming. It makes me feel safe when I feel sad."

I asked her to recall a time when she felt unsafe. Without prompting, she told me how she had been sexually and emotionally abused by her brother from the time she was eight years old. She had only ever told two people before, and both those people used the story to hurt her.

Judy's family had lived on a large dairy property and she was the middle child with four brothers. At age eight, she was coerced into the hay barn many times, where her elder brother would sexually abuse her. She knew the abuse had occurred numerous times, but couldn't be specific. Her brother had threatened that if she told anybody they wouldn't believe her anyway, so it was their secret.

From the time of the abuse, she began to put on weight. Her mother used to bake two loaves of bread every morning. Judy recalled waking up in the morning to the smell of the bread baking. For that moment every day, lying in her bed, the smell of the freshly baked bread made her feel safe and loved; she couldn't explain why, it just did. She couldn't wait to get into the kitchen and cut a huge slice of the warm bread, often going back for a second, third, or even fourth helping.

Her mother was particularly critical of her weight, constantly putting her on a diet, which included banning her from having more than one slice of bread a day. Judy hated the fact that her brothers could eat as much bread as they liked, yet her mother restricted her.

One day she finally found the courage to tell her mother what had happened with her brother. Her mother accused her of lying and making up a story as a way to get back at her brother. Judy felt the intense disappointment and hurt, and realized that nobody would believe her anyway, so she just kept the secret to herself.

At 16, Judy left home and got an apprenticeship as a hairdresser in a larger town about 500kms away.

She boarded with a family in town and they really liked her and looked after her. During her time with them, Judy lost much of her weight. She recalled that she felt loved and accepted by the family, but most of all she felt safe. When she was 18 years old, she met a boy who lived in the town. They fell in love and were married a year later.

When they were going out he was quite a romantic, compassionate person who really seemed to want to take care of her. She had told him why she ran away from home when they were going out, and she thought he understood.

But after they were married, he began to change. He started spending more time at the hotel each night drinking with his friends. He would often come home drunk and would proceed to emotionally and verbally abuse her. Many times he told her she was worthless and didn't deserve to have him, or any other man, and she was lucky that he stayed with her.

Judy and her husband had three children; a daughter and two boys. The boys, in particular, watched how their father spoke to her and began to treat her with disdain; not doing anything she asked, answering her back, and generally treating her as their father treated her.

Throughout those years, her weight began to creep on. When her husband stayed at the hotel drinking, Judy, dreading the thought of her husband's tirade on his return, would find solace by making herself three or four pieces of toast and tea at night. She could recall how the toast, with butter and marmalade, seemed to calm her, and prepare her for the tirade that would start the minute her husband walked in the door. Her subsequent weight gain over the years was another reason for his tirades.

Finally, one day Judy decided enough was enough. She packed up a suitcase and left. Her daughter came with her, the boys stayed with their father. To this day, she still has an uncomfortable relationship with her sons, who blamed her for leaving their father.

Her ex-husband eventually died from illness due to complications of alcoholism.

Over the years, Judy's weight fluctuated wildly. She would often diet, losing as much as 20 or 30 kilos, only to gain it back, and often more. The fibromyalgia symptoms began after she had contracted a bout of flu that led a period of chronic fatigue.

As we tapped, Judy kept saying, "I am worthless." "I mean nothing." "I am disgusting." "I feel so worthless." "I feel so disgusting." And finally, "Whenever I tell the truth, nobody believes me."

As we continued to tap, the intensity of each of those words increased, and we would stop and just tap on the words.

After a number of rounds, Judy just stopped and looked at me and said, "My brother took any worth from me. I was eight years old – how dare he do that!"

We tapped again another few rounds until the intensity subsided, and finally she said, "It's time I forgave him. He is dead now and died an angry, bitter man with few friends. It's actually sad. But hanging onto these angry feelings is impacting on me. I need to learn to love and value me!"

The words we tell others, and the words that are told to us, have such incredible impact. Not only was Judy dealing with the pain of the sexual and emotional abuse, but whenever she confided in others, they used her words against her.

Bread became the safety and love in her life she so desperately needed.

As Judy released the pain and emotion of the abuse and forgave her brother, her life changed.

Six months after we worked together, she messaged me to say that she was managing her symptoms well. She had managed to reduce her medication drastically, had not had a piece of bread since our session, and had begun participating in some group exercise programs that were not only helping with her energy, but had helped her begin to make new friendships. She was losing the weight she had put on and was feeling happier than she had in many years.

She was very adamant in telling me, "You know for 70 years I told myself I was worthless and not worthy of love – now I feel so joyous. Those words were not my truth – they started because of the pain my mother felt. My father verbally and emotionally abused both her and my brothers. They were simply doing what they needed to do to feel safe around him. And I understand that now. I feel very at peace. "

(If you have experienced sexual, emotional, or physical abuse, please contact either Lifeline, the Domestic Violence Helpline in your area, or get in touch with a qualified Health Practitioner for expert assistance and care.)

Tapping on Words or Actions That Hurt You in The Past

For this exercise, go back and look at the intentions you wrote in Chapter 4.

As you say the words just check in your mind to see if there are any words or actions that have been said to you in the past that hurt you or made you feel unworthy or undeserving of creating this intention you have set.

Try to *feel* where the emotion is in your body, and what level of intensity you believe it to be true. Write down both.

Let's start tapping:
Set-Up Statement: Even though I have been told these words that hurt me and made me feel unworthy or undeserving of creating this intention, I deeply and completely accept myself and how I feel.

Set-Up Statement: Even though I remember the hurtful words that made me feel unworthy or undeserving of creating this intention and it makes me feel (emotion), I deeply and completely accept myself and how I feel.

Set-Up Statement: Even though when I think about the words that were said to me and it makes me feel (emotion), I deeply and completely accept myself and how I feel.

EB: These words that were so hurtful.
SE: These words that made me feel unworthy.
UE: These words that made me feel undeserving.
UN: This sadness.
CHIN: This sadness from my past.
CB: These words that made me feel unworthy.
UA: These words that made me feel useless.
TH: These words that made me feel undeserving of creating this intention.

Repeat one more time and then take a deep breath and measure the level of intensity in your body.

See if you can link any patterns or memories of somebody saying words that made you feel that achieving your intention wasn't possible.

Once you are happy that the level of emotion has dropped to a 2-0 you can begin the Reframe Round.

Reframe Reclaim Round

Now imagine whatever you want to create is in your life right now. You are rewiring your beliefs, thoughts, and your actions to reflect what you want in your life. That includes acting as if it is already here!

Breathing in slowly and out slowly, see if you can create a picture in your mind of this reality and how it looks. How would you act differently, if this was already in your life? What words would you use? What actions would you take? Who would you spend time with? How would you choose to spend the moments in your day?

For this exercise also add the words and the feelings of forgiveness.

Set-Up Statement: Even though I have this memory of the hurtful words that made me feel unworthy or undeserving of creating this intention which is now (level of intensity), I choose now to forgive (person) for saying them. And I deeply and completely accept this new belief.

Set-Up Statement: Even though those words were so hurtful and have held me back from achieving intentions in the past, I now choose to forgive (person) for saying them so I can be free. And I deeply and completely accept this new belief in me.

Set-Up Statement: Even though I feel I have released much of the hurt, I choose now to be open to other limiting beliefs that may still be present so I can clear them and I choose to reclaim the beliefs that empower me and attract opportunities into my life in many ways. And I deeply and completely accept this new belief.

EB: I choose to allow myself to forgive (person) to release the hurt that is holding me back.

SE: I choose to release any and all self-imposed limiting beliefs that stemmed from these words and forgive (person).

UE: I choose to allow abundance, love, and success to flow into my life.

UN: I choose to allow forgiveness to be a part of every day of my life.

CHIN: I choose to forgive so I can be free to be me.

CB: I feel grateful for this power of forgiveness and open my heart to attract new opportunities in my life each and every day.

UA: I am so grateful for the opportunity to show forgiveness in my life every day in many ways.

TH: I choose to embrace this new feeling of abundance and love in my life right now.

The Power Pose

Now stand with your hands on your hips, feet slightly apart (you can do this physically, or just imagine yourself doing it). Imagine that you are standing in the most powerful position you can. Your shoulders are back, your back is straight. You are lifting up from the core center of your body.

Create a powerful affirmation that resonates with you. In this case, one that uses the word *forgiveness* may be most powerful for you.

Imagine that you are drawing up all the confidence, power, and knowledge you need through your feet and up into your heart. Then imagine that all that new energy and new affirmation is being distributed to every cell in your body. Keep breathing slow and deliberately. Hold this pose (or the image of this pose) for about 1 to 2 minutes, until you can feel this new energy powering in your body.

CHAPTER 8

Tapping to Release Self-Sabotage

Self-sabotage can rear its head in many different ways. In fact, while many of my clients know that they often sabotage their success, getting to the reason *why*, and releasing the pattern, can be frustrating.

Self-sabotage has many costumes − tiredness, lethargy, procrastination, anger, frustration, even overeating and drinking too much alcohol. Many times clients, who struggle to lose weight, know the right foods to eat and exercise to do, but find they consistently self-sabotage and undo all their intentions to lose weight.

Gay Hendricks, author of the book *The Big Leap,* calls it our *upper limit problem* − that part of us that is scared to shine or stand out from the crowd. So we sabotage our success because we fear we may fail. But when we discover the reasons for self-sabotage and release the belief, we can create an easy path to achieving what we want in our lives.

Jessie's Story

Jessie joined the *Reclaim You* program after seeing me speak at a networking event. As people were making appointments for strategy sessions with me, Jessie was busying herself with clearing up and slowly packing up.

I could see her out of the corner of my eye. She appeared to be waiting for the line to reduce and I just had a feeling that she wanted to talk to me without anybody else seeing her.

Once people had left and I started packing up, Jessie came over and started to ask questions.

Jessie was a very large woman, extremely well dressed and very elegant.

She asked me, "Does this tapping thing help with weight?" (The particular presentation I had done was using tapping to release stress for success.)

I answered *yes*, and then went on to explain to her that many people found they were able to lose weight with tapping. I explained the research. I also told her that many clients found they lost weight quite easily, once they released the emotion that caused overeating.

On the spot, Jessie handed over her credit card and said, "I am in!"

Jessie's initial session was booked in for the very next day; I had never had somebody commit to the program so fast before!

I asked her to bring the food that she wanted to give up to the appointment. She looked at me and said, "That would be the entire chocolate row of the supermarket!"

A whole shopping bag full of chocolate is exactly what she brought with her. I have been known to create miracles – but the impossible takes a little longer!

As we sat down and I began asking her questions for the initial intake questionnaire, Jessie started to tell me her story.

She told me of the years of emotional abuse at the hands of her father. She saw her mother as a weak woman who never stood up for her kids or herself. Her mother was finely built and very thin, and always looked nervous and often just went to bed for days at a time.

When she was 17 years old, Jessie left home to move in with her boyfriend. His parents were not happy about the situation, so they got married. Jessie was pregnant with her first child by the time she was 18.

Her husband was emotionally abusive to both her and her baby, so when her son was four years old, she left and moved in with her aunt. Her aunt was actually the first person in her life who really tried to help her, and the first person in her life she truly made a connection with. She felt safe with her aunt, a larger than life woman who loved chocolate, red wine, and a cigarette or two after dinner.

Each night, Jessie loved putting her son to bed and then joining her aunt, while they talked about life and love. She often talked about Jessie's mother, and how disappointed she was in her sister, believing that she never stood up for herself or Jessie.

Jessie felt a true connection with her aunt, far greater than the connection with her mother.

Jessie lived with her aunt for four years, and during that time went from a size 10 to a size 18 in clothing. The same size as her aunt.

As we began to tap, it was very obvious that although Jessie said she wanted to lose weight and give up eating chocolate, she really didn't. After numerous tapping rounds, she was still holding on to the chocolate, and her desire to eat it was still at a level 4 intensity.

I asked her the question, "Jessie if you gave up eating chocolate what would that mean?" She responded, "Who would love me then?"

The chocolate held fond memories of her aunt and the more she ate, the more she felt close to her aunt. She felt if she gave up the chocolate and lost weight, she would dishonor the memory of her aunt. Even though her aunt had passed away 10 years earlier. The chocolate represented so many nights, just Jessie and her aunt, and the feeling of being loved. "Chocolate has always represented love to me! That time with my aunt was so special, she made me feel special – if I give up chocolate and lose weight, who would love me then?"

Many times, when we set goals or intentions and it doesn't happen, there can be what we refer to as a secondary gain. An emotional connection to staying right in the same place we are now.

Losing weight may mean that you are no longer connected to somebody. As in Jessie's case, her relationship with food and love was connected to the memory of her aunt, and the times she felt most loved.

A secondary gain is where the benefits of having the problem outweigh the problem itself. This is often the cause of self-sabotage. Even though you truly want to achieve your intention, it may come at a cost. It may be connected to a memory where we felt connected or loved or part of a certain social group. It could be that if you change, it may cause a change in the dynamics of your relationship with your family or partner.

Before tapping on this issue, first I would like you to visualize the *you* as if you have already achieved your intention. For this exercise, create a really detailed vision of yourself.

If your vision is about you losing weight, see yourself as if you were that ideal weight right now. What are you wearing? What do you look like? What does it feel like? Really make the visualization as clear as it can be.

If your intention is to make more money, or achieve a promotion, or create a successful business, again I want you to imagine what you would be wearing. What do you look like? What does it feel like?

Who are the people surrounding you that have helped you achieve that intention?

Now I want you to imagine that there is a room full of your family and friends, and you are standing outside the room. Suddenly music starts to play and the double doors in front of you open up and a staircase is before you. As you begin to walk down the staircase, all your friends and family are standing there looking at you.

I want you to look in their eyes. What's happening? Are they all supportive of the *new you*? Are they happy and joyful for you? Or are there some people who feel threatened by the new you? Are there people in that room who are not happy for you? Can you have the same relationship with those people now as you did before you achieved that intention?

Spend some time just staying in that vision. Does it feel right for you? Do you feel comfortable? Is there a relationship that needs to change in order for you to truly achieve what you want?

Now, write down what happened. In that vision were there any feelings of not being supported? Is there a level of discomfort you feel? Is there a feeling that you will not be accepted? Will others around you support your change? Will others around you feel happy that you have changed? How will this change impact on your relationships? Is there a memory that prevents you from changing – like Jessie?

Can you remember if there were times in the past where you *self-sabotaged* because if you changed it would mean a change you were just not ready for?

Tapping on Self-Sabotage

Based on the exercise above, measure the level of intensity around the reasons why achieving your intention may cause you to sabotage your success because of a person or memory.

Try to *feel* where the emotion is in your body, and what level of intensity you believe it to be true. Write down both.

Let's start tapping:

Set-Up Statement: Even though I have been sabotaging myself in the past, I deeply and completely accept myself and how I feel.

Set-Up Statement: Even though I have this level (intensity number) belief about what would happen to my relationship with (person or memory) if I changed and it makes me feel (emotion), I deeply and completely accept myself and how I feel.

Set-Up Statement: Even though when I think about how easily I have sabotaged myself in the past, I deeply and completely accept myself and how I feel.

EB: This self-sabotage.
SE: This self-sabotage I fall into so easily.
UE: I didn't realize that this sabotage ran so deep.
UN: I have this fear that I might be rejected if I change.
CHIN: This self-sabotage because I felt scared of what might happen if I change.

CB: This self-sabotage.

UA: This fear that's behind my self-sabotage.

TH: This overwhelming fear leading to me sabotaging my success.

Repeat one more time and then take a deep breath and measure the level of intensity in your body.

See if you can link any specific patterns or memories around being uncomfortable achieving success in the past.

Once you are happy that the level of emotion has dropped to a Level 2-0 you can begin the Reframe Round.

Reframe Reclaim Round

Now imagine whatever you want to create is in your life right now. You are rewiring your beliefs, thoughts, and your actions to reflect what you want in your life. That includes acting as if it is already here!

Breathing in slowly and out slowly, see if you can create a picture in your mind of this reality and how it looks. How would you act differently, if this was already in your life? What words would you use? What actions would you take? Who would you spend time with? How would you choose to spend the moments in your day?

When you are ready, you can begin to tap.

Set-Up Statement: Even though I had this self-sabotage, which is now a level (level of intensity), I choose now to allow my success to flow. And I deeply and completely accept this new belief.

Set-Up Statement: Even though the self-sabotage is no longer a strong feeling, I choose now to imagine what life would be like if I achieved my intention. And I deeply and completely accept this new successful me.

Set-Up Statement: Even though I feel I have released this fear surrounding my success, I choose to be open to other limiting beliefs, and I choose to reclaim the beliefs that empower me, and release those that sabotage my success. And I deeply and completely accept this new belief.

EB: I choose to allow myself to embrace this new success feeling.

SE: I choose to release any and all self-imposed limiting beliefs about my success in achieving what I want.

UE: I choose to allow success to flow easily into my life.

UN: I choose to be open to all the possibilities that would allow me to be successful right now.

CHIN: I choose to believe in my success.

CB: I am now grateful for this new successful feeling, and the way in which opportunities to achieve what I want are attracted to me in many ways.

UA: I am so grateful for this new feeling of success that impacts on my choices every day.

TH: I choose to embrace this feeling of success in all aspect of my life right now.

The Power Pose

Now stand with your hands on your hips, feet slightly apart (you can do this physically, or just imagine yourself doing it). Imagine that you are standing in the most powerful position you can. Your shoulders are back, your back is straight. You are lifting up from the core center of your body.

Create a powerful affirmation that resonates with you, using one of the affirmations from the reframe round.

Imagine that you are drawing up all the confidence, power, and knowledge you need through your feet and up into your heart. Then imagine that all that new energy and new affirmation is being distributed to every cell in your body. Keep breathing slow and deliberately. Hold this pose (or the image of this pose) for about 1 to 2 minutes, until you can feel this new energy powering in your body.

CHAPTER 9

Tapping for Anger, Resentment and Forgiveness

When Elise joined the *Reclaim You* program, she was angry. You know how some people just have like a force field around them? Elise had one; you could feel it, and it made everybody feel uncomfortable.

Elise is a policewoman. Obviously very good at her job (I often thought that the criminals would be crazy to cross her!), Elise was desperate to be in a relationship.

She was 43 years old and her career in the police force was very important to her. She was a tough cookie, but the toughness of her exterior was hiding what I could see as a very kind, warm heart. She had been in a few relationships over the years, but it always ended with Elise being disappointed in the fact they were not tough or strong. She saw vulnerability as a weakness and wanted to find a man's man!

Elise's Story

Elise had grown up in a small country town in western New South Wales. Her dad was a sheep farmer and they had experienced the worst and the best of the Australian bush; fire, drought, floods, you name it, Elise's family had experienced it.

Ten years ago, Elise's father had died from cancer and she moved her mother into live with her, a decision she was beginning to regret and feel resentful for.

Her mother was in the early stages of dementia, which made caring for her harder and harder. Elise had two brothers who lived in other states. They made financial contributions to their mother's care, but seldom visited. Elise's resentment towards her mother was heightened by her brothers seemingly not caring about their mother, other than to send money.

As she was in her mid-40s, Elise was fearful that her ability to find a partner was becoming increasingly more difficult and she had fears of being an *old-maid*, caring for her mother for the years ahead.

It was making her angrier and Elise's health was starting to suffer. She knew it was the resentment that was causing it and wanted to fix it.

On our first intake session we talked about her resentment but no matter how much we tapped, it wouldn't shift. She held tightly to that resentment and could feel it deep in the pit of her stomach.

I asked Elise when she could first remember feeling resentful towards her brothers and immediately a memory jumped into her head. Elise was the eldest child, and her two brothers were 18 months and 3 years younger than her.

Elise remembered a time when they had to feed the sheep with hay bales. It had been a very long drought and water on the property was scarce. She had been out on the property with her father all day.

113

When they returned home late afternoon, she was looking forward to some cake she knew was left over from the night before. When she opened the cake tin in the kitchen, all the cake was gone. She flew into a rage blaming her brothers, only to be told by her mother that the boys were allowed eat it, as they were growing boys. Her mother defended the boys, telling her to go to her room and not to be so rude to them!

As we tapped, similar memories came up of always feeling that the boys were more important than she was. Even though Elise worked hard on the farm, it was made very clear to her that the farm would go to the boys. That she, as the girl, wouldn't inherit it. After her father died, the boys stayed on the farm and ran it for a few more years before selling it. As a result, her brothers received more money after the sale – they had stayed on the property and she had joined the police force. Her father had stipulated in his will that if they stayed on the property, they would be entitled to 40% each of the sale, 10% to her mother, and 10% to Elise. Elise felt that all the years she had worked alongside her father were simply ignored. She was devastated.

Her resentment and anger grew and intensified as we tapped. She began saying things like, "Life is so unfair." "It always happens to me." "I worked hard and they got everything." "Even now I am the one left looking after my mother!"

We continued tapping until the emotion reduced. During that time there were many tears until finally she said, "You know I have wasted so much of my life being resentful to those boys. But it wasn't their fault, it was my Dad's. I loved my Dad so much I didn't see it. The boys were just carrying out his wishes, which was the way it was in the country in those days. The girls did go off and get married, usually to another farmer, so it was assumed that the boys would take over the running of the property."

After a while we stopped and she was very reflective. Her face softened and the anger that surrounded that force field dissipated.

She began to cry softly. "I have wasted so much time being angry and resentful. It wasn't their fault. It just wasn't their fault."

To start the process of *reclaiming* ourselves, one of the first things to do is to forgive those in our lives who have made us *feel* a certain way.

Others have no power over how we choose to feel or to respond. That's what we do. In a book called *Man's Search for Meaning*, author Viktor Frankel wrote that with all the indignities and cruelties he experienced at the hands of the Nazis in the concentration camps, the one thing that his captors could not take was his mind.

And so is it with us.

Whenever we are being triggered by an emotion – frustration, anger, or resentment – it is not about what the other person does, it is the emotion they trigger within us. This is simply related back to an emotion or feeling we have not yet cleared.

It is one of the things I love about tapping most of all. Instead of being caught up in blaming others, we have the strategy that can free us and release the impact of that emotion on our body.

When we are triggered by a negative feeling or emotion, the person who triggered it often couldn't care less! But we dwell on it; let it eat at us, which impacts on our focus, our health, and our reality.

The key to *reclaiming* ourselves is to recall that back. Forgive it and those who were part of it, because hanging on to the anger and resentment does not serve us. As in Elise's case, it was impacting on her ability to attract a relationship into her life.

Elise was so angry and resentful towards her brothers when in fact it wasn't about them at all. It was about her father. She was angry at them for receiving what she didn't receive, but they were simply responding to a tradition that was in their father's genealogy. No amount of resentment that Elise felt was going to make the situation better until she forgave her father and subsequently her brothers. "I realize what I was doing. I was kind of grouping all men the same way, feeling let down and hurt and not being able to trust that they would be there for me!"

Elise's anger towards her father and brothers was like an invisible shield that prevented her attracting a partner into her life. As much as she wanted a relationship, she often ended it early and before the relationship became too serious. Elise had an underlying fear that she couldn't trust men. That eventually the people you love most will let you down!

How you respond to any circumstance is a pattern that is based on past experience. When you release the emotion around that belief you release you. You reclaim your power back, which allows you to *attract* what you want into your life.

Whenever you set an intention for something you want to attract into your life, it is already in motion. If there are patterns that keep reoccurring in your life, it simply means you have some past hurt or pain that needs to be healed. To feel anger or resentment about something that happened to you in the past does not serve you at all. In fact, the people who you are angry or resentful towards probably are not giving you a moment's thought. But the powerful thoughts and emotions that run through your mind constantly hold you back from creating the life you want.

And when you finally choose to heal it, forgive them, and release you ... it's a wonderful thing!

Tapping on Resentment or Anger and Forgiveness

In this tapping exercise, we are searching for any anger or resentment you may feel that may be holding you back from achieving what you want.

Anger is such a powerful emotion, as is resentment, and can be enough to hold you back from truly living a life of peace and happiness.

When you are looking at the intention you have set, just ask yourself, "Is there any anger I feel about events, people, or words from my past?" "Do I feel any resentment towards somebody from my past?"

If there is, measure the level of intensity of the emotion, where you feel it, and write it down.

Let's start tapping:

Set-Up Statement: Even though I have this anger or resentment that has held me back from achieving what I wanted in the past, I deeply and completely accept myself and how I feel.

Set-Up Statement: Even though I have this level (intensity number) anger about not being able to get what I want in the past, and it makes me feel (emotions), I deeply and completely accept myself and how I feel.

Set-Up Statement: Even though when I think about this anger and resentment I can feel it in my (where in your body), I deeply and completely accept myself and how I feel.

EB: This anger and resentment.

SE: This angry feeling.

UE: I didn't realize that this anger and resentment ran so deep.

UN: This anger and resentment I feel in my (where in your body).

CHIN: This feeling of anger and resentment that I have held on to for so long.

CB: This anger and resentment in my body.

UA: I can feel this anger and resentment in my (where in your body).

TH: This anger and resentment.

Repeat one more time and then take a deep breath and measure the level of intensity in your body.

See if you can link any patterns or memories around being angry for not getting what you wanted in the past, or if you are hanging on to anger or resentment to somebody or some event. And repeat the tapping if you feel the intensity rising again.

Once you are happy that the level of emotion has dropped to a 2-0 you can begin the Reframe Round.

Reframe Reclaim Round

Now imagine whatever you want to create is in your life right now. You are rewiring your beliefs, thoughts, and your actions to reflect what you want in your life. That includes acting as if it is already here!

Breathing in slowly and out slowly, see if you can create a picture in your mind of this reality and how it looks. How would you act differently, if this was already in your life? What words would you use? What actions would you take? Who would you spend time with? How would you choose to spend the moments in your day?

In this *reframe round,* once again include the word *forgiveness.*

When you are ready, you can begin to tap.

Set-Up Statement: Even though I had this anger and resentment which is now a level (level of intensity), I choose to now forgive (person/event). And I deeply and completely accept this new belief.

Set-Up Statement: Even though the anger and resentment is no longer a strong feeling, I choose now to imagine what life would be like if I could release the anger and forgive (person/event). And I deeply and completely accept this new belief in me.

Set-Up Statement: Even though I feel I have released this anger and resentment, I choose to be open to other limiting beliefs, and I choose to reclaim the beliefs that empower me, and attract opportunities into my life in many ways. And I deeply and completely accept this new belief.

EB: I choose to forgive those who have caused this anger and resentment.

SE: I choose to release any and all self-imposed limiting beliefs that have come about because of all the anger or resentment I felt.

UE: I choose to release this anger and resentment and allow forgiveness to flow easily into my life.

UN: I choose to be open to all the possibilities to allow forgiveness to flow into my life.

CHIN: I choose to believe in my ability to create what I want in my life.

CB: I am now grateful for this new feeling of freedom, and the way in which opportunities are attracted to me in many ways.

UA: I am so grateful for the release that this forgiveness gives me and the way that the Universe responds to that release.

TH: I choose to embrace forgiveness in all aspect of my life.

The Power Pose

Now stand with your hands on your hips, feet slightly apart (you can do this physically, or just imagine yourself doing it). Imagine that you are standing in the most powerful position you can. Your shoulders are back, your back is straight. You are lifting up from the core center of your body.

Create a powerful affirmation that resonates with you, perhaps from the *reframe* round.

Imagine that you are drawing up all the confidence, power, and knowledge you need through your feet and up into your heart. Then imagine that all that new energy and new affirmation is being distributed to every cell in your body. Keep breathing slow and deliberately. Hold this pose (or the image of this pose) for about 1 to 2 minutes, until you can feel this new energy powering in your body.

CHAPTER 10

Tapping to Smash the Inner Glass Ceiling

When we set an intention to create success in our lives, the process of manifestation towards success has already begun. But many women (myself included) are very adept at creating an *inner glass ceiling* that blocks success – and camouflages varied and sometimes seemingly valid reasons for blockages.

Those reasons can range from not wanting to outshine partners; to putting the kid's activities first; to not wanting to rock the boat at the office; to not wanting to outshine friends. You name it, we can come up with it.

But when we understand that it is just an *inner glass ceiling* that we have created, and when we release the belief behind it, we are free to create success without compromising any aspect of our lives.

Melissa's Story

Melissa, before having children, had a wonderful career in law. After graduating with a degree in law and business, she was quickly hired by a large, prestigious law firm.

Melissa was smart and worked hard. She was noticed by the partners of the firm, who continually gave her opportunities to expand her career. She flew business class around the world to meet with clients, always staying in 5-star hotels.

Twenty years ago, at the age of 32, she married one of the partners of the firm, whose wife had died five years earlier. He was 15 years older than her and highly regarded amongst his peers. They made the (seemingly) perfect couple.

They had two children who were now teenagers. She had worked part-time while they were younger, but now she was keen on getting back to her full-time career.

She was really enthusiastic to return to full-time work but was feeling lethargic and struggled to put the same energy into her work that she once had. She had trouble sleeping and found herself often drinking three or four glasses of wine at night. She was short-tempered with the kids and her husband. While initially supportive of her return to her career, her husband was starting to question if it was the right thing. His comments simply led to more arguments, with Melissa accusing him of not supporting her!

When Melissa came onto the program she knew what she wanted. She wanted to find her *mojo* again. She felt like she had plenty of years ahead of her, but her tiredness was impacting on her performance. She started to dread going to work, and coming home.

On all of our group calls Melissa was always first on and last off. She followed the program to the letter, completed all tasks as part of her *to do* list every day, and sat front and center at our two-day events. We had managed to reduce the intensity of a few things. She managed to control her wine intake. She had changed her workout routine to add more resistance work and was feeling better. But she still felt that she wasted time and procrastinated. There still wasn't the spark or energy in her work anymore. She knew there was something blocking it; she just couldn't figure out what it was.

During the course of the first day of our two-day event, one of the other participants was tapping on always feeling second best. That those around her always got more than she did.

At the break, Melissa came up to me and said, "I was really triggered by something that the last participant said. I felt really angry about it; can I tap next?"

Straight after the break, Melissa came to the front to tap. We started with, "I felt really angry when the last participant was tapping on always being second best. I don't know what it is, but I felt angry."

As we tapped and lowered the intensity, I asked Melissa to recall a time that she felt second best, or had to work harder than anybody else.

"Oh," she said. "All my life I have felt I had to work harder than anybody else, to get the same rewards. People think my success came easily – not at all! I just worked way harder than anybody else. Always first in the office in the morning and last to leave at night – always!"

So I asked her if she could recall the first time she felt she had to work harder than anybody else to get an award or success.

Immediately she recalled a time in the first year at school. Each week, the teacher gave out an award called *Student of the Week*. It was awarded to any child who she felt had worked their best for the week. There were 26 weeks in the school year, but there were 27 children in the class.

For some reason, Melissa was never chosen to be *Student of the Week*. Even though she was a model student who always did the very best she could. To rub salt into the wound, on the last week of school her best friend, who told her in the middle of the year that she didn't want to be her friend anymore, was awarded *Student of the Week*.

As we tapped on "Even though I never got to be *Student of the Week*, no matter how hard I tried ...." the tears began to fall. "Oh my goodness," she said. "That's not just in Grade 1 – that happened all the way throughout my school life. So many times I would work so hard, but I would always just miss out on getting the top award. Coming second, or worse not being acknowledged at all!"

"What's worse is that many of the girls who got awards when I didn't were often girls I had fallen out with! Oh, I can see the pattern unfolding. I am always the one who works the hardest; I don't make friends with women easily. I always see them as competition, and they don't like me either!"

The more we tapped, the more Melissa began to release the feelings of having to work harder than other people. The feelings of hurt when friendships broke down with women and feelings that she was never noticed.

At the end of the tapping, she sat in silence. She looked up at me and said, "That's why I am procrastinating and I am fearful of being successful. What if I lose my husband in the process? What if my best friend doesn't want to be my friend anymore? What if my sons end up hating me because I am successful? Oh, my god, I get it. I want to go back to my career, but the fear of repeating the past is causing the block."

I have seen this many times with women who want to create success in their career or in business, but seem to hit an invisible *inner glass ceiling*. It simply doesn't seem to make sense, but it is there, holding us back from taking success to the level we want.

Our own *inner glass ceiling* is simply playing out a pattern, usually from our childhood or school days. A pattern created when *not being* noticed, or not *wanting to be* noticed, created the belief that is triggered when we want to move to the next level of success in our lives.

When we release that limiting belief that holds us back, we are free to create success in all areas of our lives. Without feeling as if something has to be lost in order to achieve it.

That is why I am so passionate in working with women, because we have so much wisdom, so much experience, and are incredibly intuitive. We bring a different level of knowledge to the world. Our knowledge is most often learned the hard way, by balancing life, relationships, children, career ... and the laundry!

We know how to prioritize and multi-task. Negotiate deals, write reports, find lost homework, and deal with a broken-hearted 13-year-old who has just been dumped via text message, all before the first cup of coffee.

But, as with Melissa, there is often a pattern, formed from an event, person, or words from our past that holds us back. It's not about us. It's not *who* we are, it's simply the sum total of a series of events in our lives that created a limiting pattern of belief. That's it!

I truly believe it is time now for us to *reclaim who* we really are. We don't have to change a thing about us. But as we release any limiting beliefs, we are free to live the life we were supposed to live – before events, people, and words created the doubt, the fear, and the beliefs that created the reality we now experience.

Tapping on Procrastination or Fear
(Change the words to suit your feeling.)

For this exercise, again go back and look at the intention you created in Chapter 4 and see if there is any fear around it that may be creating procrastination or fear for you. Is it linked to a memory from the past where you were not acknowledged or were overlooked? Try to *feel* where the emotion is in your body, and what level of intensity you believe it to be true. Write down both.

Let's start tapping:

Set-Up Statement: Even though I am procrastinating, I deeply and completely accept myself and how I feel.

Set-Up Statement: Even though I have this (level of intensity) procrastination feeling, and it makes me feel frustrated, I deeply and completely accept myself and how I feel.

Set-Up Statement: Even though when I think about this procrastination I feel this frustration and anger in my (where in your body), I deeply and completely accept myself and how I feel.

EB: This procrastination makes me feel (emotion).
SE: This procrastination.
UE: I am not sure of the reason for the procrastination, perhaps it's fear.
UN: This procrastination.
CHIN: This procrastination that makes me feel frustrated and annoyed with myself.
CB: This limiting procrastination.
UA: This procrastination that is holding my success back.
TH: This procrastination.

Repeat one more time and then take a deep breath and measure the level of intensity in your body.

See if you can link any specific patterns or memories around why procrastinating may make you feel safe.

Once you are happy that the level of emotion has dropped to a Level 2-0 – you can begin the Reframe Round.

Reframe Reclaim Round

Now imagine whatever you want to create is in your life right now. You are rewiring your beliefs, thoughts, and your actions to reflect what you want in your life. That includes acting as if it is already here!

Breathing in slowly and out slowly, see if you can create a picture in your mind of this reality and how it looks. How would you act differently, if this was already in your life? What words would you use? What actions would you take? Who would you spend time with? How would you choose to spend the moments in your day?

When you are ready, you can begin to tap.

Set-Up Statement: Even though I had this limiting procrastination, which is now a (level of intensity), I choose now to be open to the reasons why I procrastinate, and I deeply and completely accept this new belief.

Set-Up Statement: Even though this procrastination is no longer a strong feeling, I choose now to imagine what life would be like if I felt totally empowered and in flow, and I deeply and completely accept this new belief.

Set-Up Statement: Even though I feel I have released this limiting procrastination, I choose to be open to other limiting beliefs, and I choose to reclaim the beliefs that empower me, and attract success into my life in many ways. And I deeply and completely accept this new belief about me.

EB: I choose to allow myself to embrace this new belief.
SE: I choose to release any and all self-imposed limiting beliefs about my success.

UE: I choose to allow success to flow easily into my life.

UN: I choose to be open to all the possibilities that would allow success to flow into my life.

CHIN: I choose to believe in my own value and worth.

CB: I am now grateful for this new belief about success and the way in which success is attracted to me.

UA: I am so grateful for the opportunities that allow me to experience success and that show up in my life every day in many ways.

TH: I choose to embrace success in all aspect of my life right now.

The Power Pose

Now stand with your hands on your hips, feet slightly apart (you can do this physically, or just imagine yourself doing it). Imagine that you are standing in the most powerful position you can. Your shoulders are back, your back is straight. You are lifting up from the core center of your body.

Create a powerful affirmation that resonates with you, perhaps using one of the statements in the *reframe* round.

Imagine that you are drawing up all the confidence, power, and knowledge you need through your feet and up into your heart. Then imagine that all that new energy and new affirmation is being distributed to every cell in your body. Keep breathing slow and deliberately. Hold this pose (or the image of this pose) for about 1 to 2 minutes, until you can feel this new energy powering in your body.

CHAPTER 11

Tapping to Release
Limiting Money Beliefs

When I first started on this tapping journey I began working on the issue of *money beliefs*. I wanted to know why money is such a challenge for many people, yet for others it comes easily.

It seems that there are three main areas that challenge us most: *weight, money,* and *relationships*. For some reason, it is difficult for many people to overcome all three, with one or more causing blocks.

But *weight, money,* and *relationships* are all key indicators that something is not working in your life. They are so powerful and connect to what we believe to be true for us. If there is a block in your life it will usually show up in one or more of those areas – or sometimes all three!

But delving into why money can be such an issue for so many people is an area I find fascinating. Having read many of the New Age books about money, the one theme that runs through them all is that money is just energy. A reflection of what you believe about yourself. Well then, why is it so hard for many people to attract money into their lives, even if they are intelligent and kind? Surely that should be enough?

We all know it isn't.

When I began studying the concept of money and tapping, I came across the work by EFT practitioner Margaret Lynch. In her book *Tapping into Wealth*, she talks about how our money issues are determined by our earliest money memories. How our parents talked about money, and what they believed about money, impact on what we believe is possible. Usually we unconsciously either honor or dishonor our parents' beliefs about money, based on how money was talked about in our home.

If you are in business, but struggling to attract enough money, first examine your earliest money memories.

What were your parents' beliefs about work and money? Were they the type of people who believed that you should get a good education, work hard, buy a house, and save hard for your retirement? If that is the case, you may find it difficult to manage the ups and downs of entrepreneurship.

Were your parents the type of people who worked hard all their lives, but only managed to scrape by by being frugal? Then you may subconsciously believe that you are *dishonoring* your father by making more money than he did or by taking risks and setting huge targets.

Have you spent your whole life trying to prove to your parents that there was another way to make money? That you wanted to break the boundaries and do something that proved you were right? You may be trying so hard to be successful, but with a subconscious fear that perhaps they were right all along!

Or perhaps you are like one of my clients Susan who, like me, has a family generational history of money made and lost throughout the years.

Susan was a member of a multi-level marketing group. We met at a networking event and liked each other immediately and had so many similar stories to share. We got talking one day about how different we were from our mainstream upbringing. How we loved the ability to be in charge of our destiny.

One day she said, "You know, I always feel as if there is a sense of foreboding just around the corner. Like I can never seem to relax when it comes to money."

Susan, like me, grew up in a religious family and went to an all-girls school. Unlike me, she went on to university where she studied journalism. She worked as a journalist for a while before commencing a career writing technical manuals and books for different organizations. When her children were small, she got involved with a multi-level marketing company and had managed to create a great income from that business.

One day, we were comparing our family histories when it came to money. We discovered that we both had stories of wealth, made and lost, in our family history.

My mother's family had experienced many cycles of wealth, followed by financial hardship. My great grandfather was a renowned entrepreneur and, also unfortunately, a gambler. My great grandmother turned whatever spare money she could into pieces of jewelry so my great grandfather couldn't gamble it!

The family had hotels for many years. My grandmother went to university to study pharmacy, but had to leave when times became tough to help with the family business. The family wound up living in New Guinea. My grandmother eventually met my grandfather on a holiday, and after a brief courtship and wedding returned to New Guinea, where my mother together with six other children, were born. My mother used to talk glowingly about her idyllic childhood and her love of the country and its people. That life changed suddenly when the Japanese invaded New Guinea in 1942, and the family was hurriedly evacuated, forced to leave everything behind. The family resettled in Queensland and even with the support of family, struggled to make ends meet. With two more children now bringing the total to nine, my mother left school in Year 9 so she could go to work to help the family financially.

My father's story of wealth and struggle was similar. His ancestor, Col. George Johnston and his wife, a convict, Esther Abrahams, arrived on one of the ships of the First Fleet, arriving in Australia in 1776. Over the years, they amassed a great deal of land and wealth that disappeared over the generations through poor investment and family feuds.

Prior to the Depression, my grandfather owned a store and bakery in country Victoria. However, the drought and depression in the 1930s forced him to relocate his young family to Melbourne. However, jobs were scarce and times were tough. Raising five children who were all educated at Catholic schools meant money was always tight.

Consequently, both my parents were very conservative with their money. They insisted on us getting a good education and were careful with their money and their investments.

In talking with Susan, it was very obvious for both of us how our own money challenges came about. We had both grown up in families that had experienced the best and worst of entrepreneurship. We could see how our money beliefs eventuated. Being safe, having a good job, and having a regular income was much safer than having money and losing it.

The die was cast for our beliefs. And as Susan said, "No wonder I have this sense of foreboding when I think of money – that's the history of our family. No matter how much you make, something is bound to happen where you could lose it."

If you struggle to attract money into your business or life, then examining your earliest money memories can be a powerful exercise.

When I am doing a presentation on tapping and abundance this is always a hot button. Especially when people begin to examine their genetic history around both the making and the keeping of money. Our genetic history having a huge impact on our beliefs now.

In his groundbreaking book *The Biology of Beliefs,* Dr. Bruce Lipton summarizes that human beings can control gene activity and rewrite it by focusing on our beliefs. And that our beliefs, whether positive or negative, do not just exist in our minds, but are also directed from our cellular makeup. What is interesting in this is that tapping has been shown to change our belief structure at that cellular level – remember when I talked about that *Apex effect* earlier? If you can find the genetic pattern, handed down to you throughout the generations, perhaps you can rewire the genetic belief that has created your money reality now!

So first, see if you can find out any generational patterns of money in your family. See if you can make a correlation between the money beliefs of your parents, and their parents and grandparents.

Next is to examine the *tail-enders* you have around money. Often times those come from phrases you may have heard as a child. So for this exercise, write down as many phrases as you can remember that were used when you were growing up about money. There may even be a few you still use!

For each statement, measure the level of intensity of belief from 0-10, and tap on each one until your level of intensity around the statement is zero. Try to think of as many of these phrases as you can.

Here are a few to get you started:

- *Money doesn't grow on trees.*
- *Money is hard to come by.*
- *Money is the root of all evil.*
- *Money doesn't make you happy.*
- *You have to save for a rainy day.*
- *Money can't buy happiness.*
- *We may not have money, but we have love.*
- *We have to wait for our ship to come in.*
- *Saving is hard.*
- *Money just slips through my fingers.*
- *I never know where my money goes.*

If you have more, also write them down and tap on each of them.

How do You Honor or Dishonor Your Parents' Beliefs About Money?

Next, examine if you are either honoring your parent's beliefs about money – or you feel as if you are dishonoring them. Or perhaps you are just working hard to prove that they are wrong!

In all cases, money is just energy. But if you have any negative feelings or beliefs it can be enough for you to create that *confirmation bias* around the issue of money. If your belief runs deep, you will continue to recreate the pattern around money – no matter how hard you try!

When you are ready to release those feelings, your ability to make and keep money will grow exponentially.

Here are some of the statements that can help you create tapping scripts around money:

- *My earliest memory around money was ....*
- *My parents' beliefs about money were....*
- *My current beliefs about money are ....*
- *My current money situation is....*
- *My past history with money has been ....*
- *My feelings about money are ....*
- *I would like my money situation to be ....*

Tapping on Money Beliefs

For this exercise, try to recall a moment when you can remember money being discussed in your home. Or at the very least, a time when you felt money was an issue in your family.

134

Try to *feel* where the emotion is in your body, and what level of intensity you believe it to be true. Write down both.

Let's start tapping:

Set-Up Statement: Even though I have this (intensity number) feeling about money, I deeply and completely accept myself and how I feel.

Set-Up Statement: Even though I have this (intensity number) belief about money and it makes me feel (emotion), I deeply and completely accept myself and how I feel.

Set-Up Statement: Even though when I think about this belief I feel this (emotion) in my (where in your body), I deeply and completely accept myself and how I feel.

EB: This belief makes me feel (emotion).
SE: This (emotion) feeling.
UE: I didn't realize that this belief ran so deep.
UN: This (emotion) feeling.
CHIN: This belief that makes me feel (emotion).
CB: This limiting belief.
UA: This (emotion) feeling.
TH: This (emotion) belief.

Repeat one more time and then take a deep breath and measure if the level of intensity in your body has lowered to a 2-0.

Now try to recall a memory when money was discussed, or you could recall a time when money was an issue in your family.

135

Measure the level of intensity again and do another tapping round if it has increased.

Once you are happy that the level has dropped to a 2-0 you can begin the Reframe Round.

Reframe Reclaim Round

Now imagine whatever you want to create is in your life right now. You are rewiring your beliefs, thoughts, and your actions to reflect what you want in your life. That includes acting as if it is already here!

Breathing in slowly and out slowly, see if you can create a picture in your mind of this reality and how it looks. How would you act differently, if this was already in your life? What words would you use? What actions would you take? Who would you spend time with? How would you choose to spend the moments in your day?

When you are ready, you can begin to tap.

Set-Up Statement: Even though I had this limiting belief about money, which is now a level (level of intensity), I choose now to reframe my belief about money, and I deeply and completely accept this new belief.

Set-Up Statement: Even though the limiting belief about money is no longer a strong feeling, I choose now to imagine what life would be like if money flowed easily into my life. And I deeply and completely accept this new belief.

Set-Up Statement: Even though I feel I have released this limiting belief about money, I choose to be open to other limiting beliefs, and I choose to reclaim the beliefs that empower me and attract money into my life in many ways. And I deeply and completely accept this new belief.

EB: I choose to allow myself to embrace this new belief.

SE: I choose to release any and all self-imposed limiting beliefs about money.

UE: I choose to allow money to flow easily into my life.

UN: I choose to be open to all the possibilities that would allow more money to flow into my life.

CHIN: I choose to believe that money flows to me in many ways.

CB: I am now grateful for this new belief about money, and the way in which money is attracted to me.

UA: I am so grateful for the abundance that shows up in my life every day in many ways.

TH: I choose to embrace abundance in all aspect of my life right now.

The Power Pose

Now stand with your hands on your hips, feet slightly apart (you can do this physically, or just imagine yourself doing it). Imagine that you are standing in the most powerful position you can. Your shoulders are back, your back is straight. You are lifting up from the core center of your body.

Create a powerful affirmation that resonates with you, perhaps choosing a statement from the *reframe* round.

Imagine that you are drawing up all the confidence, power, and knowledge you need through your feet and up into your heart. Then imagine that all that new energy and new affirmation is being distributed to every cell in your body. Keep breathing slow and deliberately. Hold this pose (or the image of this pose) for about 1 to 2 minutes, until you can feel this new energy powering in your body.

CHAPTER 12

Tapping on Feeling Invisible and Overlooked

Karyn joined the *Reclaim You* program because she wanted to make money and be successful. She was able to achieve just about every other goal she set for herself, but not this one.

"I set myself a goal to lose weight this year, and I lost 10kg. I set myself a goal to run a half marathon and I did. I even set myself a goal to go overseas, and I ended up winning a trip! But when it comes to creating more money or more success in my life, everybody else around me seems to be able to do it, and I can't. I just can't figure out what is going on."

As we started to tap, I asked Karyn what emotion she felt when she said the words, "I never achieve my goal to be successful and make more money." Immediately she said, "I feel so angry; in fact, I can feel the anger in my stomach – and it's a level 8 or 9."

So we started tapping on just the anger until she could feel the shift and it came down to about a level 4.

Karyn's Story

I asked Karyn what she was angry about. She told me that there were many times when people she worked with, or had helped, had gained a promotion or an award and she was never even acknowledged by them.

"I seem to have all these great ideas about how to help others, and they take the suggestion and run with it – and I am left with nothing. What is that?"

I asked Karyn to recall a time when she could first remember that happening. Immediately she recalled a time in her early career where she was working as an assistant manager in a franchised store. Her boss was younger than she was and, at first, she really liked him. They had a positive and honest relationship and she was happy to be the assistant manager and learn as much as she could from him.

After a few months, it became very obvious that the manager of the store was extremely disorganized. He wasn't good with managing staff and was unpredictable in his emotions. He often became annoyed with staff for the smallest things. He would disappear for hours at a time during the day, often taking extra days off, leaving Karyn to run the store when he wasn't there. The longer she was there, the more he delegated to her.

At first she didn't mind, as she saw it as a way to up-skill herself. But eventually she began to resent the extra hours she was doing without any further increase in her pay.

At the company's annual awards dinner, Karyn's store was nominated for *Store of the Year* and her boss was nominated as *Manager of the Year*. The second title frustrated Karyn a little as she knew that she was the reason her boss looked so good!

At the awards dinner, not only did her store win, but her manager was given a separate award for *Excellence in Staff Training*.

Karyn sat at the table in shock and anger as her manager accepted the award and thanked his whole team. In his speech, he talked about how hard he worked and that hard work eventually pays off.

As she told the story, while tapping, she could feel her anger rising. So we continued to tap on the anger she felt when she had done all the work and her manager won the award.

The more we tapped the more memories came to her mind. "This has happened so many times in my life. I seem to attract the jobs I want, but I end up doing all the work and other people look good because of me. It's happening right now with the company I am with. One of the people I work closely with was just awarded *Employee of the Year*. She is successful in what she does because I provide her with the information she needs to do her job! It's not fair, nobody ever notices me. I do all the work and no matter what I do I just feel invisible, like no matter how hard I work it's not enough!"

I asked Karyn if she could remember the first time she ever felt like that. She looked straight at me and said, "My Dad – nothing I ever did was good enough. I remember a time when I was in about Grade 4 I think. I wanted Dad to listen to my spelling because I had learned all 10 words that were set for homework. So I wrote the 10 spelling words on a piece of paper. But I wanted them to look perfect, so I rubbed them out each time I thought the words were not written out perfectly enough. When I handed him the paper, he told me that he could see the eraser marks and to do it again. I was only giving him the paper so he could listen to my spelling!"

The patterns of our past continually show up in our present reality. If you feel invisible and overlooked, instead of dwelling in the emotion, try to link where you first felt like that. Every action we take now is based on a belief we have about ourselves that is usually etched into our memories at an early age.

Karyn's overwhelming anger at being overlooked and feeling invisible in her current role began with her father's reaction to those spelling words.

We continue to repeat the patterns we know and we are comfortable with. Karyn's pattern of trying to please people in high positions and seeking out acknowledgement from them was something she subconsciously kept playing out. She was then disappointed when it wasn't forthcoming. Her father only focused on the eraser marks on the page, when she was looking for praise from him because she had learned all her spelling words.

Right there, at that moment, the pattern was laid down. *No matter how hard I work, nobody sees me or acknowledges what I have done.*

It wasn't until we could tap to reduce the emotion around the belief that we could find the story that was holding the pattern in her life.

Tapping on Feeling Invisible and Overlooked

For this exercise, go back and look at your intentions.

As you read the intention out loud, just check your level of emotion around achieving success in the past. Was there ever a time when you felt invisible or overlooked? Was there ever a time when you felt that others around you gained more than you did? Is there a feeling that others seem to be successful and you have to work harder than anybody else?

Try to *feel* where the emotion is in your body, and what level of intensity you believe it to be. Write down both.

Let's start tapping:
Set-Up Statement: Even though I feel like I never achieve success and have to work harder than anybody else to be noticed, I deeply and completely accept myself and how I feel.

Set-Up Statement: Even though I have this (level of intensity) belief that success for me is hard to get, and it makes me feel (emotion), I deeply and completely accept myself and how I feel.

Set-Up Statement: Even though I never seem to be able to achieve success when everybody else around me can and sometimes I just feel invisible, I deeply and completely accept myself and how I feel.

EB: Everybody else can create success but not me.
SE: I feel angry because it's so hard for me.
UE: I feel so invisible.
UN: This anger and frustration at feeling invisible.
CHIN: Others achieve success, but I don't.
CB: This anger and this frustration.
UA: I feel angry when I look at this intention.
TH: I have to work harder than anybody else.

Repeat one more time and then take a deep breath and measure the level of intensity in your body.

See if you can link any patterns or memories, like Karyn's, to your pattern now.

Once you are happy that the level has dropped to a 2-0 you can begin the Reframe Round.

Reframe Reclaim Round

Remember now to imagine whatever you want to create is in your life right now. You are rewiring your beliefs, thoughts, and your actions to reflect what you want in your life. That includes acting as if it is already here!

First hold your hands over your heart.

Breathing in slowly and out slowly, see if you can create a picture in your mind of this reality and how it looks right now. How would you act differently, if this was already in your life? What words would you use? What actions would you take? Who would you spend time with? How would you choose to spend the moments in your day? Your subconscious does not know the difference between what is reality now and what is yet to be reality.

Set-Up Statement: Even though I had this uncomfortable feeling, which is now a (level of intensity), I choose now to step into my own success. And I deeply and completely accept this new belief.

Set-Up Statement: Even though I still have a little of the anger, I am ready to release it and step into my own success and power and release the need to seek acknowledgement from others. And I deeply and completely accept this new belief in me.

Set-Up Statement: Even though I feel I have released this anger and frustration, I choose to be open to other limiting beliefs, and I choose to reclaim the beliefs that empower me and attract success into my life in many ways. And I deeply and completely accept this new belief.

EB: I choose to allow myself to embrace this new successful feeling.

SE: I choose to release any and all self-imposed limiting beliefs about my success and visibility.

UE: I choose to allow success to flow easily into my life.

UN: I choose to be open to all the possibilities that would allow success to flow into my life.

CHIN: I choose to believe I am capable of creating success in my life.

CB: I am now grateful for this new success feeling, and the way in which opportunities are attracted to me in many ways.

UA: I am so grateful for the success that shows up in my life every day in many ways.

TH: I choose to embrace this new successful feeling in all aspect of my life right now.

The Power Pose

Now stand with your hands on your hips, feet slightly apart (you can do this physically, or just imagine yourself doing it). Imagine that you are standing in the most powerful position you can. Your shoulders are back, your back is straight.

Create a powerful affirmation that resonates with you, perhaps choosing a statement from the *reframe* round.

Imagine that you are drawing up all the confidence, power, and knowledge you need through your feet and up into your heart. Then imagine that all that new energy is being distributed to every cell in your body. Hold this pose (or the image of this pose) for about 1 to 2 minutes, until you can feel this new energy powering in your body.

CHAPTER 13

Tapping on Comparing Yourself to Others

We live in a wonderful time right now where we can be digitally connected to people all over the world. Social media has created a whole brave new world, where we are able to be part of other people's success, events, and lives.

With two children living in another country and one in another state, I just love that I can communicate with them often, and in real time, via technology.

However, social media can also come at a cost. We are also living at a time when people tend to share the *best of their lives* online, keeping the *worst of their lives* to themselves.

As my social media friend Mari Smith says, "We have to be mindful of not comparing our worst day with somebody else's best day."

We all have a chosen path to success, but events, people, or words can pull us out of our own genius.

Comparing ourselves to others often starts at a very early age. Your birth order, or the competition for one parent's love or attention, can be the beginning.

Many of us grew up in highly competitive school environments, where being the fastest runner or the top football player or the top academic performer was so important.

The teenage years are particularly competitive as the pecking order of *cool kids* and *geeks* and *losers* can make life feel so challenging. Many teens spend their time trying to fit in, being cool, and generally navigating the world.

But as we get older, we may often continue silently comparing ourselves to others. Questioning if we are good enough or smart enough, which can stop you from truly being successful.

Our challenge is not to be better than anybody else. Our challenge in this noisy, competitive, social media world is to simply be the best version of ourselves – not anybody else – in love with *who* we are and being open to the opportunities that continue to present themselves to us.

Darleen's Story

Darleen is a 40-year-old woman who works in an extremely competitive real estate office. She has been selling real estate for over 15 years, and has received many top sales person awards during that time.

Recently, Darleen has been struggling with debilitating back pain. She had seen a physiotherapist, a chiropractor, and had been receiving regular acupuncture treatments, as well as undergoing massage therapy. While initially she felt some relief, the pain would inevitably return.

After a presentation I gave to a women's networking group, Darleen approached me to ask if tapping could help with the pain. I explained some of the research around tapping and pain, but explained that to truly get to the bottom of it often requires more than one session.

After a conversation to see if I could help, Darleen joined my next eight-week program.

On our first intake session together, I could tell that Darleen's pain was causing her a great deal of discomfort. So prior to beginning, I asked her if she wanted to tap to see if we could get the intensity of the pain down.

After a tapping round on just the pain in her lower back, it lowered a little, but we couldn't seem to get it below a level 5 intensity.

So I asked her to share with me when she felt the pain at its worst.

"It always seems to start about mid-afternoon and is particularly bad most nights. I don't have it on the weekends usually, only during the week. Perhaps because I am not sitting at my desk as often."

I asked her to tell me when the pain first started. The only thing she could remember was that it started about 18 months ago. She first noticed it after she had worked continuously for 10 days without a break.

We continued tapping and I asked her to tell me what was going on during those 10 days, and why she had worked so long without a break.

Darleen had been the top sales person in the office for five years in a row and then a new sales woman joined the team. Darleen couldn't explain why this woman seemed to get under her skin. But from the moment she started, Darleen felt her position as the top sales person was under threat.

I asked her to describe the woman to me. She used words such as untrustworthy and manipulative to describe her. She couldn't understand why people seemed to like her; she was obviously only out for herself and not a team player at all.

I asked her if she could recall a memory from her past when somebody else made her feel like that.

At first she couldn't, so we just continued to tap on how this new sales girl made her feel. After a few rounds her eyes became wider and she began to recall a memory.

147

She suddenly remembered a girl from her last year of primary school. The year prior, Darleen was part of the touch football team that had won the premiership and she was awarded best player of the year. As this was her last year of junior school, Darleen really wanted to be selected in the top touch football team. She also secretly had her heart set on being the captain.

At the beginning of the term a new student came to the school and joined the practices and tryouts for the team. At each practice, Darleen noticed that this girl was always positioning herself close to her. Somehow everywhere she turned, this girl was there. She wouldn't pass the ball to other players and was always seeking ways to score a try.

To make things worse, this girl always seemed to hang around the coach after practice, asking how she could improve and always offering to pack up the equipment. The coach seemed to take an instant liking to the new girl.

Darleen could see exactly what she was doing and that made her even more determined to play better and train harder. But nothing she seemed to do was better than this new girl and often times after practice Darleen would go home in a foul mood.

On the day of the team announcements, the new girl not only made the team, but was appointed captain, and Darleen vice-captain. Darleen was devastated.

As the year went on, Darleen picked up most of the work that the captain should have done. The new girl always seemed to have excuses why she had to leave practices early. She could never stay to help pack up the equipment.

The disharmony in the team was obvious, and the team lost most of its games and didn't make the finals.

Darleen said, "No matter how hard I tried, I couldn't get the coach to see how this girl was manipulative. She wasn't as good a player as I was, nor was she team captain material at all. But she had a way of pulling the wool over everybody's eyes."

148

As we tapped, Darleen began to make the connection between the girl at school and the new girl in the office, and could see the pattern.

After three or four rounds of tapping Darleen said, "I get it. Both those girls stopped me believing in myself. Instead of just getting on and doing what I am good at, this new sales girl made me feel I had to do something or be something more than I already am! When I was in that team at school I tried too hard – it's exactly what I am doing now!"

We tapped on another round, using Darleen's words of *never feeling good enough; working hard and not being noticed;* and *feeling manipulated.*

I asked Darleen to check on the pain in her back; it had completely disappeared.

As we begin the process of *reclaiming who* we really are, the need for being any more than we already are disappears.

If you are constantly comparing yourself to others or living in a state of competitiveness, you are out of your own creative flow.

We are *enough*. We are already our best. We can strive to do better, but only better than *who* we were or *what* we were doing the day before – not trying to be better than somebody else.

Excellence is a habit. Like setting yourself daily tasks to meditate, workout, tap, journal. To read something that inspires you or educates you. Making the decision to eat well, go to bed earlier, drink less alcohol, or eat less sugar. Choosing to connect with people who inspire you, who support you, and encourage you. At the same time releasing those who want you to remain the same or find fault in what you do.

Those are the keys to staying in flow and creating success. Each of those requires us to add a little extra effort each day. Challenging the intensity of your workout. Adding an extra weight or an extra repetition to your exercise routine. Choosing to read a new self-help book rather than watch TV, or challenging yourself to stretch your meditation time. Those are the things that you can expand and improve on. And in turn they return you – to you!

When we focus on somebody else's story, we lose sight of our own.

When you set your intentions for what you want, then focus to release any limiting beliefs that hold you back, you move into that state of *flow*. That's when the manifestation flows into your life as well. Whatever you need will come to you in many different costumes, but always as opportunities to create success. If you get pulled into somebody else's story, you may just miss them!

Tapping on Comparing Yourself to Others

For this exercise, check to see if you fall into the habit of comparing yourself to others. Either in your work environment or perhaps in your family.

Try to *feel* where the emotion is in your body, and what level of intensity you believe it to be. Write down both.

Let's start tapping:

Set-Up Statement: Even though I find myself comparing myself to others, I deeply and completely accept myself and how I feel.

Set-Up Statement: Even though I have this (level of intensity) belief about not being good enough and it makes me feel that I am not as good as others, I deeply and completely accept myself and how I feel.

Set-Up Statement: Even though when I think about this belief, I feel this doubt and feel as if I am not good enough in my (where in your body), I deeply and completely accept myself and how I feel.

EB: This belief makes me feel (emotion).
SE: This comparing feeling.
UE: Sometimes I just don't feel I am good enough.
UN: This competitive feeling.
CHIN: This (intensity number) belief that makes me feel (emotion).
CB: This limiting belief.
UA: This (emotion) feeling.
TH: This competitive belief.

Repeat one more time and then take a deep breath and measure the level of intensity in your body.

Once you are happy that the level has dropped to a 2-0 you can begin the *Reframe Round*.

Reframe Reclaim Round

Now imagine whatever you want to create is in your life right now. You are rewiring your beliefs, thoughts, and your actions to reflect what you want in your life. That includes acting as if it is already here!

First hold your hands over your heart.

Breathing in slowly and out slowly, see if you can create a picture in your mind of this reality and how it looks right now. How would you act differently, if this was already in your life? What words would you use? What actions would you take? Who would you spend time with? How would you choose to spend the moments in your day? Your subconscious does not know the difference between what is reality now and what is yet to be reality.

Set-Up Statement: Even though I had this limiting belief where I was comparing myself to others, which is now a (level of intensity), I choose now to reframe my belief about myself and my confidence in my abilities. And I deeply and completely accept this new belief.

Set-Up Statement: Even though the limiting belief of not being good enough is no longer a strong feeling, I choose now to imagine what life would be like if I believed I was the best me I could possibly be. And I deeply and completely accept this new belief.

Set-Up Statement: Even though I feel I have released this limiting belief about myself and my abilities, I choose to be open to other limiting beliefs, and I choose to reclaim the beliefs that empower me, and attract opportunities into my life in many ways. And I deeply and completely accept this new belief.

EB: I choose to allow myself to embrace this new belief.
SE: I choose to release any and all self-imposed limiting beliefs about my own abilities.
UE: I choose to allow confidence to flow easily into my life.
UN: I choose to be open to all the possibilities that would allow confidence and a strong belief in me to flow into my life.
CHIN: I choose to believe I am perfect just the way I am.
CB: I am now grateful for this new belief about my confidence and the way in which opportunities are attracted to me.
UA: I am so grateful for the confidence that shows up in my life every day in many ways.
TH: I choose to embrace this new feeling of confidence in all aspect of my life right now.

The Power Pose

Now stand with your hands on your hips, feet slightly apart (you can do this physically, or just imagine yourself doing it). Imagine that you are standing in the most powerful position you can. Your shoulders are back, your back is straight.

Create a powerful affirmation that resonates with you, perhaps choosing a statement from the *reframe* round.

Imagine that you are drawing up all the confidence, power, and knowledge you need through your feet and up into your heart. Then imagine that all that new energy is being distributed to every cell in your body. Hold this pose (or the image of this pose) for about 1 to 2 minutes, until you can feel this new energy powering in your body.

CHAPTER 14

Seeing the Mirror, Understanding the Lesson

Each and every relationship in our lives is a reflection of what we believe, what we feel, what we need to clear, or what we need to learn.

Our internal world is reflected into our external world. People show up in our lives to help us evolve to our highest purpose, to teach us how to truly be an expression of love. Our most treasured and dearest family and friends allow us to express that love, each and every day. The most basic of human needs is to love and to be loved in return. That's it! It doesn't get much more complicated than that.

When we feel loved, our confidence rises. We feel safe to be our truest self and to live our highest purpose. But when love is absent in our lives in some way, we live in shattered pieces. We are one person when we are with those we feel safe with, another with those we don't. When we are with those who shatter us, our energy drops and our thoughts become distracted. We get pulled out of flow and into something else that does not allow our true self to express.

Many of us have that one person in our lives who causes us some grief. It may be a child, a parent, a sibling, or a friend. That one person whose job it seems to be to remind you that as much as you think you are evolved and spiritual – you still have some work to do!

However, the answer to any problem we have in our relationships with others is always within us. We determine how we are going to respond. That response is simply a reflection of our emotions or feelings at the time.

How another person makes you feel, is your call.

When we spend so much time being frustrated or angry about what somebody else does, that feeling pulls us out of our flow. It holds us back from staying focused, with those feelings of frustration taking up valuable creative brain space!

The problem for many of us is that we get caught up in the drama. How they make you feel, instead of taking a step back and asking, "What's going on for me right now? What do I need to clear?"

I have mentioned before in other chapters that while we cannot control people or events in our lives, we can control how we respond to them.

In all relationships, the feeling *we* get from the relationship is always about us – never about the other person. In order to achieve our intentions in our lives, we also need to take responsibility for everything that happens in our lives. That includes our responses to others – even if they are causing you grief or heartache. The question to always ask is, "What part am I playing in this reality? What is going on in me that I need to clear, so I can change this pattern?"

When you take 100% responsibility for your emotions and feelings, you gain the power back within you. Other people's issues, reactions, responses are none of your business. When you understand why you respond the way you do, that's when you can change it. By continually clearing those blocks that hold you back from experiencing love, happiness, and success in your life.

Ariella's Story

Ariella was the eldest of six children and grew up in the suburbs of Sydney. Her family was a large, rambunctious, noisy, loving, emotional Italian Catholic family.

Her parents migrated to Australia during the 1950s, with two suitcases and 50 pounds in their possession. They settled in Sydney and worked hard to raise all the children, sending them to Catholic schools, and created a new life in Australia.

Ariella was married at 21, and she and her husband Tony went on to have three sons. Ariella loved the fact that her sons were growing up surrounded by a large, extended family. They experienced many wonderful, memorable, noisy dinners and family celebrations. Her mother was a superb cook and consequently every family event involved lots of food and wine.

Ariella loved getting together with her family, but her relationship with her middle sister had begun to change. Her middle sister was very judgmental and exceptionally critical of everybody and everything. Lately, Ariella began to feel as if her sister was exceptionally critical and judgmental of her.

Ariella often shared her frustrations with Tony. While originally he was supportive, lately his responses were that she was like that with everybody and to stop getting upset about it. She shared her concern with another sister, who felt the same as Tony. She also felt that Ariella was overreacting and that she should just ignore her sister, like everybody else in the family did.

So at our two-day event, when I shared the concept that when somebody *pushes our buttons* it is simply a clue that something within us needs to heal, Ariella volunteered to tap to see if it could shift her responses to her sister.

I asked her to explain how her sister's judgmental behavior made her feel. "I just feel so criticized by her; that my opinions don't count and she is so overbearing. She makes me feel so small and insignificant at times, like I am not as smart or pretty as she is. That I am not as good a mother as she is. I just always feel like I am being judged, and I can't be myself. It is just so frustrating!"

So first we did a round on her feeling frustrated and judged, until the intensity of that emotion came down a little. I then asked her if she could remember a time in her life when she felt judged and she wasn't as pretty or smart as somebody else.

We kept tapping as Ariella thought for a while. After a while she said, "I don't know if this memory is relevant. But I remember when we were at school, my mother used to pack us Italian lunches – salami, mortadella, and often on sourdough bread. They were always very strong smelling and the other kids often turned their noses up when I was eating lunch. No matter how many times I pleaded, my mother would never buy vegemite or bread from the supermarket for us. I just wanted to be like the other kids. I don't know why I am thinking about this now, but I remember one day, perhaps I was about six, one of the popular girls told me that I was just a poor immigrant and I should go back to Italy, or eat proper foods like Australians did."

I asked Ariella to measure the intensity of that emotion and how it made her feel. "Right now the intensity is really high, like an eight or nine. I felt like I was always being judged anyway – and this girl, who was pretty and popular just made me feel so small and insignificant. I remember feeling like in order to fit in to the school I would have to stop being the Italian girl and start acting like the Australian girls."

As we tapped on each of the feelings that the six-year-old Ariella felt, she began to connect the same feelings as when her sister judged her. "My sister has always had a much better relationship with my mother than I do – for no other reason than they both love to sew clothes. I was always out doing things, but my sister would spend lots of time with Mum doing what they liked – shopping for fabric, creating patterns, etc. Even though

I didn't like to sew, I was always a little jealous of my sister's better relationship with Mum. And she could get away with way more than I ever could!"

As we continued to tap, Ariella could feel the intensity around her sister's judgment drop. Finally after a few rounds she said, "You know what, I just realized that I am actually really dismissive of her. I don't ask her about her work or take anything more than a glance at any of her sewing! I just realized it is actually me who is the judgmental and dismissive one!"

So I asked Ariella what she felt when she thought of her sister – immediately she felt as if her sister had it so much easier than her.

"I was a little resentful of the fact that she was small and cute and popular with friends. My parents were harder on me than they were on her. I had to work harder than her at everything. But I think I have made the connection. She always wanted to hang around me and when I think back to it, I was actually quite mean to her. I can remember telling her that she wasn't to hang around with me or my friends, and to go get her own, mostly because I was jealous that they might like her more than me. I feel a little ashamed of that actually!"

Any adverse reaction or feeling that we have towards others actually holds a clue. Where in your life have you been like Ariella – judgmental and dismissive? Because the thing that most drives us crazy about somebody is usually the thing that most drives us crazy about ourselves. That person just shows up in our lives for us to clear whatever emotion or block we have. When we clear that emotional intensity within us, we clear the emotional response we have. When you clear the emotion, your relationship changes – not because the other person changes, because you do.

When we release the emotional triggers, it frees us up to live in that flow of love, non-judgment, compassion, and joy. Our vibration lifts, our intuition flows freely, and staying focused on what we want in our lives becomes so much easier.

Tapping on Feeling Judged by Others

For this exercise think of the person who you feel judged by. Write down how they make you feel when they are judging you. As with Ariella – do they make you feel small? Do they make you feel frustrated? Angry? Sad? Emotional?

Next, try to *feel* where the emotion is in your body. Is it in your stomach? Your heart? Your head? Then measure the level of intensity on a scale of 1-10 (10 being the highest intensity) and write it down.

Let's start tapping:

Set-Up Statement: Even though I have this (intensity number) feeling because I feel so judged all the time by (person), I deeply and completely accept myself and how I feel.

Set-Up Statement: Even though I have this (intensity number) feeling in my (where in your body) about being judged, and it makes me feel (emotion), I deeply and completely accept myself and how I feel.

Set-Up Statement: Even though I have this (emotion) feeling in my (where in your body) whenever I think about how (person) makes me feel, I deeply and completely accept myself and how I feel.

EB: This (emotion) feeling.
SE: This uncomfortable feeling.
UE: I hate this feeling of being judged.

UN: This (emotion) feeling of constantly being judged.

CHIN: This intense feeling of (emotion) because I never feel good enough.

CB: This intense feeling of (emotion).

UA: I feel so judged all the time.

TH: This overwhelming feeling of being judged and dismissed.

See if you can link any patterns or memories around being judged in the past. (If not, just continue tapping on the feeling.)

Repeat one more time and then take a deep breath and measure the level of intensity in your body.

Once you are happy that the level of emotion has dropped to a 2-0 you can begin the Reframe Round.

Reframe Reclaim Round

Now imagine whatever you want to create is in your life right now. You are rewiring your beliefs, thoughts, and your actions to reflect what you want in your life. That includes acting as if it is already here!

First hold your hands over your heart.

Breathing in slowly and out slowly, see if you can create a picture in your mind of this reality and how it looks right now. How would you act differently, if this was already in your life? What words would you use? What actions would you take? Who would you spend time with? How would you choose to spend the moments in your day? Your subconscious does not know the difference between what is reality now and what is yet to be reality.

Set-Up Statement: Even though I had this judged feeling, which is now a level (new level of intensity), I choose now to be aware of, and release, any judgments I have of others. And I deeply and completely accept this new belief.

Set-Up Statement: Even though being judged by (person) is no longer a strong feeling, I choose now to forgive and to send love and compassion to (him/her) and to myself for all the times I have judged others. And I deeply and completely accept this new way of thinking.

Set-Up Statement: Even though I have released the intensity of feeling judged, I choose to be open to other limiting beliefs, and I choose to reclaim the beliefs that empower me, and attract opportunities into my life in many ways. And I deeply and completely accept this new belief.

EB: I choose to allow myself to be me.

SE: I choose to release any judgments I have of others.

UE: I choose to allow love, compassion, and forgiveness to flow in my life every day.

UN: I choose to be open to expressing love and forgiveness always.

CHIN: I choose to release any judgments of others.

CB: I am now grateful for the love, joy, and compassion that shows up in my life always.

UA: I am so grateful for the beautiful relationships that I attract into my life in many ways.

TH: I choose to embrace this way of being in all aspects of my life right now.

The Power Pose

Now stand with your hands on your hips, feet slightly apart (you can do this physically, or just imagine yourself doing it). Imagine that you are standing in the most powerful position you can. Your shoulders are back, your back is straight.

Create a powerful affirmation that resonates with you, perhaps choosing a statement from the *reframe* round.

Imagine that you are drawing up all the confidence, power, and knowledge you need through your feet and up into your heart. Then imagine that all that new energy is being distributed to every cell in your body. Hold this pose (or the image of this pose) for about 1 to 2 minutes, until you can feel this new energy powering in your body.

CHAPTER 15

Tapping to Release Self-Sacrifice and Embrace Self-Care

For many women, the habit of sacrificing ourselves and our needs for others is a habit that can be difficult to break. There can be a fine line between *serving* others and *sacrificing yourself* for others. The balance can be tenuous, but the difference can make a huge difference to your health, your energy levels, and your ability to manifest success, health, and happiness in your life.

When you become crystal clear on what you want to manifest in your life, there are often times when what *you* want has to come first. The juggling act, however, can be made even worse if you are always putting others first and your needs last.

As a recovering *self-sacrificer*, it has been a long journey for me. I am pretty sure it was a belief handed down to me from generations of women before me, so I don't think it was something I just made up!

As women, when we are growing up, we are often given mixed messages. On one hand we are encouraged to do whatever we want. On the other hand, there seems to be an unspoken expectation that we can do what we want, as long as we do that *after* we have cared for everybody else first.

My self-sacrificing behavior began at a very early age. I attended an all-girls Catholic school and the message that was constantly, and perhaps unconsciously, shared was that sacrificing your needs for others was something you aspired to.

We were told many stories about the saints and how virtuous they were because they were poor and worked to serve others. In contrast, those who were rich and indulged were sinners!

Somehow in all of that, I adopted a belief that in order to be a good and saintly person sacrificing myself for others was for the greater good! And that working for the common good of all was something to aspire to.

So I went above and beyond the extra mile all the time; so far past it, in fact, it could be called the extra marathon!

But the thing was, I was okay with it. In fact I loved telling everybody how hard I worked and how much I did. I reveled in my self-sacrificing belief as if it was an Academy Award! My belief in my value and my worth was tied up in *what* I did – not *who* I was.

For most of my life I wasn't even aware I had this disempowering belief – I just thought it was expected of me.

My pattern of self-sacrificing behavior was both obvious and invisible.

I would go to work when I was sick, believing that whatever I had to do for my employer was more important than caring for my own health. I worked long hours and took on an unsustainable amount of extra responsibility, without extra pay, for the greater good of the organization. In fact, one year I was the only employee left in the building late one Christmas Eve, as we had a printing deadline to meet and I took that on as my sole responsibility, long after everybody else had left for their holidays.

When we devalue and dishonor our own worth, that belief expresses outwards. We send a subconscious message to the universe that we do not value ourselves. So that is what we receive. Events and people in our lives will reflect what we believe. In every career you have, there will always be the boss who loads you up with extra responsibility and without extra pay. Certain friends will never call to see how you are. Your kids will continue to leave the kitchen untidy or expect you to bail them out financially, without a thought to how that impacts on you.

How others treat you is a direct reflection of what you believe about yourself and what you believe you deserve.

It took a serious health scare for me to realize that I had run out of options. The need to sacrifice myself for others needed to be released. It was the day that my relationship with myself, with others, and with life changed.

I had been working in a school for 10 years. I loved the role, but worked exceptionally long hours wearing *busy* as that badge of honor I referred to earlier.

Often there by 7:30 in the morning, I could be there until 10 at night if there was a function. Weekend work was expected, I took very little time off (in fact when I resigned I had over six weeks of sick leave accrued). I very seldom took a lunch break and prided myself on being able to juggle the various roles and expectations. I had asked numerous times for an assistant, always being told there was no money in the budget. So I pulled on my *self-sacrificing and carry on regardless* nature and continued the relentless and punishing expectations.

One day it all came to a grinding halt. I had been feeling exhausted for many weeks. I was struggling to find the energy to work out; I would come home some nights and need to have a nap before dinner started. I was cranky with the kids and Gerry. I just felt rundown. But we were right at a busy time in the school year and things needed to be done. I just ignored the tiredness, hoping that I would eventually get over it.

One day I arrived at work at 7:30am and there were already six people at my office door. Even before I had a chance to put my handbag away they began to ask me questions. Now, usually, I prided myself on being able to balance all expectations. Nothing was ever too difficult and no problem too challenging to overcome.

A member of the parents' committee was the last one in line. She started asking me a question about something. I could see her mouth move, but I couldn't make sense of what she was saying. It was as if my brain was totally scrambled. All I could muster was, "I have no idea, sorry, I am not feeling well. Can I get back to you?"

I picked up my handbag and told the receptionist that I had to go home. As I drove home I just started to cry uncontrollably. I was exhausted. I got home, went upstairs, fell onto the bed and slept for five hours.

When I woke, I phoned my naturopath and surprisingly she had an appointment free the next morning at 9:00.

"You are suffering from adrenal fatigue," she said. *Adrenal what?* I thought, I had never heard of it before. While it was not widely recognized within the mainstream medical community, when she read out all the symptoms and the causes it was exactly what I was experiencing. Trouble getting out of bed; chronic tiredness, even after you wake up in the morning; trouble thinking clearly or finishing tasks. All brought on by long periods of extreme stress.

She said, "You have some decisions to make. This level of extreme stress can lead to chronic health problems. It is simply unsustainable."

Two days later I resigned.

But it wasn't until I began tapping that I began to see the cause of the breakdown. While it happened in that job, it was a pattern that I carried out my whole life. It didn't matter which job I was in, I had always worked longer hours than most others and took on way more responsibility than was needed.

It also carried over to my relationship with the kids. I would ask them to do something, and if they didn't do it in my timeframe, or the way I wanted, I would do it myself. I could hear my own words in my head: *If you want it done right you have to do it yourself. Nobody around here helps me. I have to do this by myself. Nobody notices how much I do.*

I could remember words that I grew up with: *Life wasn't meant to be easy. Think of others before yourself. What makes you think you're special?* Each of those statements reinforced the belief that I had to put others first. Solidly embedding the belief that I needed to sacrifice myself for others – even though I didn't realize it was a belief. I just thought it was a way of being.

My pattern for that self-sacrificing belief was laid down during my school days and impacted throughout my whole life. Once I realized that the pattern was there, I knew I had to clear it. Not only for me, but it was a belief I did not want to pass on to my daughters.

One of the things I love so much about tapping is that you can do that. When you clear a belief or pattern for you, you also clear it for the generations to come – because you change how you do things; how you see things; and how you respond to events. By clearing the pattern in me it has stopped me unconsciously passing that belief onto my children.

Tapping has allowed me to release that need to self-sacrifice, so I no longer feel I have to do that in order to value myself. Today, I am healthier and happier than I was 20 years ago. My energy levels have stabilized, my relationship with both my husband and kids has improved, and I honestly feel I am ageing backwards! All because I now understand how important my own self-care is. My health and wellbeing comes first – it is a priority, not an option!

I still work long hours, but this time it is in my own business which I just love! When I work with clients I feel energized. There is a wonderful balanced giving and receiving of energy, so rather than feeling tired, I feel inspired!

Self-care is what replaces self-sacrifice. It is imperative to realize that as women, as mothers, as wives, and as daughters, the more we care for our own wellbeing, the more present we can be to those we love the most. The quality of the time we spend with others is far more powerful than the quantity of time. And the quality of that time is dependent on your mental, emotional, and spiritual health that will flow when you adopt a model of what I like to call *exquisite self-care*.

Exquisite self-care goes beyond the occasional massage or time out. It includes rethinking all areas in your life where you are not experiencing a *balanced giving and receiving of energy*. Reviewing every activity or person in your life, and evaluating the impact they have on your energy levels. In doing so, understanding the lesson they hold for you and why they are present in your life. Re-evaluating where you place your time and attention. Most importantly releasing any beliefs you have around self-sacrificing yourself for others. Otherwise the self-care will never feel whole. You will always feel as if you are grabbing moments, feeling as if you deserve it, rather than joyously embracing the *exquisite self-care* that is essential to your life each and every day.

Tapping to Release the Need to Sacrifice Yourself for Others

Ask yourself the question, "Where in my life do I sacrifice my needs for others?"

Write a list of all the times you put others' needs ahead of your own, where you feel that there is an imbalance of energy.

Next, try to *feel* where the emotion is in your body. Is it in your stomach? Your heart? Your head? Then measure the level of intensity on a scale of 1-10 (10 being the highest intensity) and write it down.

Let's start tapping:

Set-Up Statement: Even though I have this (intensity number) feeling because I know I have spent so much of my life sacrificing myself for others, I deeply and completely accept myself and how I feel.

Set-Up Statement: Even though I have this (intensity number) feeling in my (where in your body) about the times I have sacrificed myself for others, and it makes me feel (emotion), I deeply and completely accept myself and how I feel.

Set-Up Statement: Even though I have this (emotion) feeling in my (where in your body) whenever I think of how often I have put my needs last, I deeply and completely accept myself and how I feel.

EB: I sacrifice myself for others all the time.
SE: It is such a pattern in my life.
UE: I am not sure I can break it.
UN: What if I stopped doing it, how would others react?
CHIN: Just thinking of this makes me feel (emotion).
CB: This intense feeling of (emotion).
UA: I have sacrificed myself for others all my life.
TH: This overwhelming feeling of (emotion).

See if you can link any patterns or memories around the times you have sacrificed yourself for others, and it left you feeling drained, sad, or angry. (If not, just continue tapping on the feeling.)

Repeat one more time and then take a deep breath and measure the level of intensity in your body.

Once you are happy that the level of emotion has dropped to a 2-0 you can begin the Reframe Round.

Reframe Reclaim Round

First hold your hands over your heart.

Breathing in slowly and out slowly, see if you can create a picture in your mind of how releasing the need to *self-sacrifice* would feel. How would you act differently, if you released that belief and instead chose to adopt allowing *exquisite self-care* times for you?

What words would you use? What actions would you take? Who would you spend time with? How would you choose to spend the moments in your day? Your subconscious does not know the difference between what is reality now and what is yet to be reality.

Set-Up Statement: Even though I sacrificed myself for others so many times, I choose now to be comfortable and confident in creating *exquisite self-care* times for me. And I deeply and completely accept this new belief.

Set-Up Statement: Even though the (emotion) has come down, I am not sure how I can release this belief and pattern, but I am willing to begin the process. And I deeply and completely accept this new belief in me.

Set-Up Statement: Even though I have released the intensity of sacrificing myself for others, I choose to be open to other limiting beliefs, and I choose to reclaim the beliefs that empower me, and attract opportunities into my life in many ways. And I deeply and completely accept this new belief.

EB: I choose to allow myself time to put me first.

SE: I choose to release any and all self-imposed limiting beliefs about it being OK to put myself first.

UE: I choose to feel at peace in creating some me time.

UN: I choose to be open to all the possibilities to create more *exquisite self-care* time for me.

CHIN: I choose to begin loving and honoring myself.

CB: I am now grateful for all the new ways in which I can honor and love myself.

UA: I am so grateful for the knowledge that shows up in my life every day in many ways.

TH: I choose to embrace this way of being in all aspects of my life right now.

The Power Pose

Now stand with your hands on your hips, feet slightly apart (you can do this physically, or just imagine yourself doing it). Imagine that you are standing in the most powerful position you can. Your shoulders are back, your back is straight.

Create a powerful affirmation that resonates with you, perhaps choosing a statement from the *reframe* round.

Imagine that you are drawing up all the confidence, power, and knowledge you need through your feet and up into your heart. Then imagine that all that new energy is being distributed to every cell in your body. Hold this pose (or the image of this pose) for about 1 to 2 minutes, until you can feel this new energy powering in your body.

CHAPTER 16

Learning to Trust – Tapping to Embrace Intuitive Eating

In order to help your intentions become reality, learning how to trust your intuition – your gut feeling – is important and powerful.

For women in particular, our intuition is our most powerful ally. But, many of us do one simple thing each and every day that takes away our ability to trust our intuition. We dishonor the messages the body sends us when making food choices.

Understanding this put me back on my own journey towards honoring the value and power of my own intuition. It was simply a matter of re-learning how to trust my own body and stop obsessing about good and bad foods.

Every day, we are bombarded by many messages about health and nutrition. Each decade it seems there is another new, different, and better way to eat. In the 1970s it was the *Pritikin Diet*. In the 1980s it was the *Atkins Diet*. In the 90s it was all about *Low Fat* diets. Today, it's now *Paleo* and *No Sugar* diets. There is always new research pointing to something we didn't know before.

The diet industry in the USA totaled $64 billion in 2014, and Australians spent $613.6 million in 2015 on diet or weight-loss products. But at the same time, both these countries report that up to 1 in 3 adults could be considered overweight or obese.

It's clear something isn't working.

When I am working with clients, one of the processes I teach is how to trust their intuition in making their food choices. It was a skill that healed my food and weight obsession and also helped me hone my intuitive skills that support me in so many other ways.

Here is My Story

I began a career in the fitness industry in Canada in 1981 (or as my children like to remind me – last century!). I had met my husband Gerry in late 1979, and in 1980 moved from Australia to start a life together in Canada.

But I had a secret that people knew nothing about and a move to Canada made the secret even more challenging.

From the age of about 15, I had an extremely unhealthy obsession with my weight. Bordering on bulimia, I ran up to 10 kilometers (6 miles) each day, as well as taking diet pills and laxatives right through to my early 20s. I would weigh myself twice a day. The number on the scales determined how far I ran, how many diet pills I took and, sadly, how I would feel about myself for the rest of the day.

When I moved to Edmonton, I was concerned about how I was going to keep running when the winter temperature often dropped to -30C!

In expressing my concerns to a friend at work, she told me about an indoor exercise class with music, held at the YMCA. So in late November 1980, I took myself off to attend my very first aerobic dance class.

Oh gosh, I just loved it. The class movements were pretty basic by today's standards, but wow, it was fabulous.

Soon one class led to four classes a week. I wanted to know all about this aerobic dance and how it worked, so I became an instructor.

Within months, Gerry and I started an aerobic dance company. I was learning as fast as it was growing and we were soon trailblazing this brand new area.

That first class was the beginning of a 15-year career, before another major life event caused a change in direction when the word *autism* entered our lives. (I wrote about our autism journey in the best-selling book *David's Gift: Asperger's Syndrome, Life & Love*. You can find it on Amazon.com.)

While I loved the fitness industry, my secret obsession still dominated my life.

There was a constant battle going on in my head. I had a *magic* number that dictated my ideal weight − 47 kilos (103 pounds)! I was very restrictive in the foods I would allow myself to eat. No white bread products, no fat, and no sugar and I taught four to five classes a day.

My husband Gerry, on the other hand, is a naturally thin person. In fact, in the 35 years I have known him, his weight has not shifted more than a couple of kilos.

Gerry has always eaten anything he wants. He has no regard for how many calories, fat grams, carbohydrates, etc.; rather, he goes simply by what he feels his body needs to eat.

When we first met, I used to think he was nuts. His favorite meal at the time was a prime rib of beef served with baked potatoes swimming in butter, sour cream, bacon bits and chives on the top. (Wow, how things have changed − Gerry and I are both now vegetarians/dairy-free and eat no sugar!)

But whenever he would have that meal, I would have the same thing, but without the butter, sour cream, and trimmings. He thought I was nuts!

One day, he asked me why I didn't have sour cream. My reply was simply, "It's fattening!" feeling very justified in my knowledge, and superior in the fact that he obviously didn't read the books!

He then slowly picked up a teaspoon and dipped it into the sour cream. He held up the spoon in front of me and said, "How could a teaspoon of sour cream put on a pound of weight?"

I got up from the table in a huff, saying that he didn't know what he was talking about. He had never had a weight problem in his life. I, on the other hand, had to battle with my weight all my life – so what would he know! (Ever notice how self-righteous you can become around people who are thinner than you – especially when the conversation gets around to food.)

I walked into the kitchen, stood by the sink, and looked out the window. He was right, that made sense. How could a teaspoon of anything put on a pound of weight? That was physically impossible. What on earth had happened to me? I knew in my heart he was right, even though in my head I believed differently.

Gerry honestly believed that he could eat anything and never put on weight. But the way he ate was also different. He took time. He prepared food on his plate as if it was going to be photographed. If he wanted a cookie – he would take one out of the jar, put it on a plate, make himself a cup of coffee, sit down, open the newspaper and proceed to read. He would take a bite of the cookie and a sip of coffee. Then put both down until he was ready for the next sip and the next bite

(In that same period of time I would have eaten half the packet of cookies, waiting for the kettle to boil!)

I realized I had lost the art of tasting and enjoying food. I had also put food into *good and bad* categories. If I ate *good foods*, then I was a *good* person; if I ate *bad foods*, then obviously I was a *bad* person. I had little concept of feeling full and always made sure I finished every piece of food on the plate, whether I felt full or not.

I really wanted to believe I could eat anything I wanted as well. I loved anything to do with personal development. At the time, I was reading anything I could about how to change your mind-set and beliefs.

So I figured out that if I said something to myself enough times, I could change the way I thought. And I was determined that I was going to change!

So I got some small cards and wrote the words *I now allow myself to eat anything I want. I choose to honor my body.*

I put the cards everywhere. Inside the pantry door, in the shower, on the dashboard of the car, in my purse, by my bed, anywhere I could see them a few times a day.

It took about six weeks before I noticed significant changes. (If I had known about tapping then, it would have happened in six days!) Small at first, but slowly the obsession towards food began to change. If I wanted a piece of cake, I ordered it. Many times, I would surprise myself by leaving half on the plate, simply because I didn't *feel* like anymore. That, in itself, was a huge shift.

As I began the process of allowing myself to eat what I wanted, I began to see the patterns unfold. I realized that food (or lack of it) filled a gap. That I often chose food to mask an emotion rather than feeling it. I also began to really connect what emotions triggered certain food binges. I noticed if I felt sad or unloved, I tended to reach for chocolate. If I was angry or frustrated, I would reach for chips or salty crackers as if the crunch of the food satisfied the feeling I couldn't express. As my intuitive choices became more of a habit, I began to learn to both honor how I felt and be okay with how I felt. Rather than eating the feeling away!

Once I learned to become an *intuitive* eater, my body changed and my energy changed. Most importantly, I began to trust my intuition more for everything from food to business decisions.

As women, our intuition is our most powerful asset. Whenever I ask my clients where they sense their intuition – most say *in my gut!*

Gut feelings can be very powerful. How many times have you had a *gut feeling* about something that flew in the face of common sense, and your *gut feeling* prove to be right? Perhaps it helped you make more money, created a new opportunity – or saved your life?

But, if you deny that most basic of intuitive messages – the one that tells you what your body needs – then how do you trust your intuition for the most powerful questions of your life?

Your intuition is your early warning system that helps you to ask the right questions and listen to the right answers, particularly on the days when you feel challenged. That *knowing* – the one that just feels right.

Today, I work with women who have decided that enough is enough. They are over the dieting game and want to learn to get in tune with their bodies and what they need.

Instead of taking six weeks to do it (as it did with me), with tapping they are able to release food cravings and understand why they have certain emotional responses to food almost instantaneously. When they get in touch with their feelings and their body again, the dieting rat race stops.

Tapping to Become an Intuitive Eater

Ask yourself, "What if I believed it was possible for me to become an intuitive eater?" "What if I allowed myself to totally trust my intuition to make the choices?"

Now measure the *feeling* in your body when you ask the question.

Is there a feeling of fear? Could you trust yourself? Is there a feeling of disbelief that it couldn't possibly work? Whatever the thought or feeling, write it down.

Where do you *feel* the emotion? Then measure the level of intensity on a scale of 1-10 (10 being the highest intensity) and write it down.

Let's start tapping:

Set-Up Statement: Even though when I think of the possibility of embracing intuitive eating I feel this fear, I deeply and completely accept myself and how I feel.

Set-Up Statement: Even though I have this (intensity number) feeling in my (where in your body) about the thought of not dieting, and allowing my body and intuition to make the choice, and it makes me feel (emotion), I deeply and completely accept myself and how I feel.

Set-Up Statement: Even though I have this (emotion) feeling in my (where in your body) whenever I think about just trusting my intuition to make the choices, and I am scared I might put on weight, I deeply and completely accept myself and how I feel.

EB: This (emotion) feeling.
SE: I feel (emotion) when I think of eating intuitively.
UE: I don't think I can trust myself.
UN: This (emotion) feeling that makes me so uncomfortable.
CHIN: This feeling of (emotion) at the thought of eating intuitively – what if I get fat?
CB: What if it doesn't work.
UA: I don't think I can trust my intuition, what if I am wrong.
TH: This overwhelming feeling of (emotion).

See if you can link any patterns or memories around how food has impacted on your life. The times in the past when you felt out of control, or you felt like you had failed at losing weight in the past. (If not, just continue tapping on the feeling.)

Repeat one more time and then take a deep breath and measure the level of intensity in your body.

Once you are happy that the level of emotion has dropped to a 2-0 you can begin the Reframe Round.

Reframe Reclaim Round

First hold your hands over your heart.

Breathing in slowly, see if you can create a picture in your mind of this reality and how it looks right now. How would you act differently, if you ate intuitively all the time? What words would you use? What choices would you make? How would you choose to spend the moments in your day?

Set-Up Statement: Even though I had this uncomfortable feeling, which is now a level (new level of intensity), I choose now to be comfortable and confident, allowing myself to eat anything I want, and trust in my intuition. I deeply and completely accept this new belief.

Set-Up Statement: Even though the words *I now allow myself to eat anything I want, I now honor my body* feel a little scary still, I deeply and completely accept this new belief in me.

Set-Up Statement: Even though I have released the intensity of fear around trusting my intuition, I now choose to be open to other limiting beliefs, and I choose to reclaim the beliefs that empower me, and attract opportunities into my life in many ways. And I deeply and completely accept this new belief.

EB: I choose to allow myself to eat anything I want; I honor my body at all times.

SE: I choose to allow myself to eat anything I want; I honor my body at all times.

UE: I choose to allow myself to eat anything I want; I honor my body at all times.

UN: I choose to allow myself to eat anything I want; I honor my body at all times.

CHIN: I choose to allow myself to eat anything I want; I honor my body at all times.

CB: I am now grateful for the way my body chooses foods that enhance my energy, vitality, and confidence.

UA: I am so grateful for the way in which the food I choose creates vibrant health and energy.

TH: I am so grateful for the way my body responds to this new way of eating, and I choose to trust my intuition always.

The Power Pose

Now stand with your hands on your hips, feet slightly apart (you can do this physically, or just imagine yourself doing it). Imagine that you are standing in the most powerful position you can. Your shoulders are back, your back is straight.

Use the powerful affirmation *I choose to allow myself to eat anything I want; I honor my body at all times*

Imagine that you are drawing up all the confidence, power, and forgiveness you need through your feet and up into your heart. Then imagine that all that new energy is being distributed to every cell in your body. Hold this pose (or the image of this pose) for about 1 to 2 minutes, until you can feel this new energy powering in your body.

CHAPTER 17

Tapping on the Habit of Being Busy

O ne of the things that will stop an intention coming to fruition is simply being too busy.

We have become a planet that is obsessed with, and addicted to, the notion of being *busy*. Women, in particular, tend to wear being busy like a badge of honor. Wrapping up their sense of *who* they are and seeking to find purpose in a daily, long *to do* list.

Often the addiction to being busy actually hides an issue far greater than the inability to fit everything into one day. Rather it has more to do with hiding a deeper feeling of loss of purpose.

Many times throughout this book I have referred to the importance of being aware of the opportunities that present themselves to you. The minute you create an intention that is truly aligned with you, your *Higher Self* focuses your awareness to the opportunities that can make that intention a reality.

The problem is often the opportunities are not going to be so obvious as to hit you on the head. They are, instead, often incredibly subtle; perhaps a thought, a word, an idea, or a feeling. It is here that you need to be attuned to your most powerful skill − your own intuition − to understand and recognize the message.

We are human beings, not human doings. But in the focus of the *to do* list and the franticness of life, the ability to listen to your own intuition can be lost.

We were all born with the infinite knowledge required to create success, love, joy, and happiness in our lives. But over the years, events, people, and words that hurt us, disempower us and we begin to doubt.

So starts the cycle. The doubt causes us to create self-imposed limitations which then create new patterns and soon we rewrite a new story. Suddenly we have a new way of being, often so different from the original one we were meant to play out.

We stop listening to our intuition because we don't trust it. The hurt and disempowerment creates a disruption to our inner knowing. We begin to buy into the new story at the same time, seeking a return to what we knew to be true from the beginning, but not knowing how to get there.

I have seen this over and over again with clients when tapping. When the heaviness and darkness of the limiting beliefs are shifted, many comment that they feel whole again. Their connection to both themselves and a power far greater than them connects once again. I have seen people appear years younger; their faces and bodies look lighter as they release the heaviness of a limiting belief. It's as if the light of their true spirit returns.

Tapping simply helps you *reclaim you*. The *who* you were before the events, people and words of the past caused you to doubt *yourself,* to doubt what you knew to be true when you came to this planet, fully embodied with your spirit and soul.

You came here to love and to be loved, with the innate knowledge on just how to do that.

That is what happens when we begin this process of reclaiming the *who* we really are. We begin the journey of *reclaiming* the love and the knowledge we were born with, releasing beliefs that no longer serve us, rewiring the patterns, and rewriting the story of our lives. Operating from our true soul guidance.

But, when our world is filled with stuff to *do*, we miss it. We miss the little hints that our intuition is trying to tell us, because we don't hear it, and even if we do, we often don't trust it. The intuitive clues we need are always there, because we get glimpses of ideas or memories or gut feelings that keep playing themselves out in our heads.

Those fleeting thoughts hold the key; we just have to be present enough to hear them and choose to act on them.

Marissa's Story

Marissa joined the program after I had spoken at a businesswomen's breakfast. She was a *tiger mom* on steroids! (Her words, not mine.)

Marissa had grown up as an only child in a family of outstanding high achievers. Her mother had a degree in law, and worked in merchant banking. Her father was a surgeon at one of the largest teaching hospitals in the Asia Pacific Region.

Marissa was dux of her year at one of the top girl's schools in the country. As well as being able to play numerous instruments, she was also fluent in four languages.

Her parents adored her but had scheduled almost every single waking hour of her day as a child. If it wasn't tutoring, it was music lessons or language lessons. Her parents had very strict guidelines about who she could associate with and vetted most of her friends.

After school, she went on to graduate with First Class Honors in International Business and found work for a large international corporation. She loved nothing more than to have her day scheduled from 5am to 10pm, with a digital diary keeping her on track.

She met her husband James, a successful civil engineer, and they had two daughters within three years.

Marissa set the same punishing schedule for her daughters as she had experienced as a child. Her daughters attended an exclusive private school and had weekly music and language lessons. Marissa spoke to them in English, Mandarin, and French on a regular basis.

Everybody's days were organized, and Marissa loved nothing more than the feeling of having everybody's schedules down to the last minute.

But lately, Marissa was starting to feel that there was something wrong with the way things were unfolding.

Her youngest daughter, who was 12 years old, was beginning to rebel. She didn't want to continue music lessons, but instead wanted to take up soccer. Marissa saw soccer as a complete waste of time. She wouldn't let her daughter go to practice, instead picking her up every afternoon and supervising her homework and music sessions. Every night, her daughter would scream at her about how much she hated her.

To make things worse, James was siding with their daughter. Suggesting that Marissa needed to take a step back and let their daughter do what she wanted.

Marissa was not having any of it. She remembered being 12 years old and telling her mother she didn't want to practice piano. Her mother ignored her and sat with her every night to make sure she completed an hour of practice. As far as Marissa was concerned, her daughter's desire to stop learning piano, and play soccer, was fanciful. Now, Marissa was very grateful to her mother for guiding her though those times she wanted to give up, and as a result she was a proficient pianist who loved playing to entertain friends and family.

To overcome the screaming matches, Marissa simply added more things on her *to do* list. She knew that the busier she was,

184

the less impact her daughter's hurtful words would have on her. So she simply threw herself more into her work.

When Marissa came to the two-day event, she pulled me aside and said, "You know, everybody here has so many problems; I don't and I feel a bit like a fraud being here." I asked her why she came and she said, "So I could find a way to increase my energy levels so I can keep up with all the things I have to do in a day."

So after the last break on the last day, I asked Marissa if she would like to tap on how to create more energy in her day. She jumped at the chance.

I asked her to measure her energy levels on any given day. Her response was about a level 6 or 7 and she would love to get that to a level 9 or 10, so she could fit more into her day.

I asked her to tell me of an issue or a person who made her feel low in energy. She immediately said, "The arguments I have with my daughter – they just drain me, and they are so unnecessary. The fact that my husband thinks my daughter is right is something that really makes me angry; actually, that's probably worse, come to think of it."

So first we tapped on the anger she felt when her husband sided with her daughter, and the level dropped from a level 8 to a level 4 in a very short round. She could feel her energy increase as the anger dissipated.

I then asked her to think of the arguments with her daughter and measure the level of energy again. This time she said, "Oh my, I can feel my energy levels drain when I think of the arguments." I asked her what emotion she felt when she thought of the arguments with her daughter. She said, "She is so ungrateful, she just doesn't understand how much work it takes to keep everybody on task and fit what we have to do in a day – these are for her own good and she will, like me, be so grateful to her mother one day because I didn't give in!"

I asked how her daughter's ungratefulness made her feel, and she said, "Like my opinion is not of value, and I don't know what I am talking about."

I then asked her if she could remember a time in her past when she felt like her opinion was not of value and she didn't know what she was talking about.

She was quiet for the longest time, and finally she looked at me and said, "My mother made me feel like my opinion wasn't of value." I asked her to recall a specific incident when she felt her opinion wasn't of value.

She replied, "I remember it so well – I was about six years old. I was given an invitation to attend a sleepover for one of the girls in my class. It was her birthday, and she had invited everybody in the class – there were only 12 of us. My mother wouldn't let me go. No matter how many times I asked, how many tears I shed, my mother didn't believe in sleepovers. On the night of the party, my mother arranged a dinner party at our home and I had to play for the guests. At school the next Monday, all the girls were talking about the party. They had face painting, a pony, and each of the girls was given a set of fairy wings. They had all brought the fairy wings to school to wear at lunchtime. I remember being devastated. So instead of going into the playground, I went into the music room, locked the door, and practiced the piano the whole lunchtime. I just pretended to be busy so I didn't feel so left out."

It was one of those moments where the entire room fell silent; everybody got it, including Marissa. We continued to tap on how the six-year-old Marissa felt at being left out. How being busy playing the piano at lunchtime helped hide the tears and the pain; how she felt her mother didn't honor or value her own feelings.

"You know," she finally said, "the funniest thing is that I have thought of that memory a lot lately, especially after arguments with my daughter. But I was putting my mother hat on. I tried to convince myself that my daughter would eventually understand that not letting her give up piano would be a good thing. I was thinking about this from my perspective, not my daughter's. I just realized how much that hurt, how left out I felt, and how being busy stopped me feeling the hurt. I am doing the same thing to my daughter; I am not honoring what she wants. How can she learn to trust her intuition if I don't let her both do what she wants and then learn from that decision, whether it be the right one or not?"

One of the greatest gifts we give anybody, including ourselves, is the gift of honoring who we really are. Who knows if it is the right thing or the wrong thing for Marissa to allow her daughter to give up the piano to play soccer? We don't, but what we know to be true is that when we continue to carry the pain of our past into our children's lives we dishonor the *who* they are.

That is what I love so much about tapping. When we clear our own pain, we set our children free to create their lives in their own light, not ours. Our role is to support them, nurture them, and create the boundaries for them. But most of all, to love them with a pure heart. To listen to our intuition to know what feels right, and to help them listen to, and to trust in, their own intuition that will guide them for the rest of their lives.

Tapping on Learning to Trust Your Intuition

This tapping exercise is all about releasing any blocks you may have that would be impacting on your ability to trust your own intuition. In particular, if you are feeling overwhelmed or life just feels so busy, and you may be feeling a little like you are on a hamster wheel!

Now measure the *feeling* in your body when you think of that overwhelm.

Next, try to *feel* where the emotion is in your body. Is it in your stomach? Your heart? Your head? Then measure the level of intensity on a scale of 1-10 (10 being the highest intensity) and write it down.

Let's start tapping:

Set-Up Statement: Even though I have this (intensity number) feeling because I feel so overwhelmed and busy, I deeply and completely accept myself and how I feel.

Set-Up Statement: Even though I have this (intensity number) feeling in my (where in your body) because I am so overwhelmed and busy and I know I am not listening to my intuition at all, and it makes me feel (emotion), I deeply and completely accept myself and how I feel.

Set-Up Statement: Even though I have this (emotion) feeling in my (where in your body) whenever I think about this incredible overwhelm and how busy I am, I deeply and completely accept myself and how I feel.

EB: This (emotion) feeling.
SE: This overwhelm.
UE: I just feel so overwhelmed with life.
UN: This (emotion) feeling of constantly being busy and overwhelmed.
CHIN: This intense feeling of (emotion) because I feel so disconnected from my intuition.
CB: This intense feeling of (emotion).
UA: I am not sure how to stop feeling so overwhelmed.
TH: This feeling of overwhelm disconnecting me from my intuition.

See if you can link any patterns or memories around a time when perhaps being busy stopped you from doing what you really wanted, or it felt safer to be busy, rather than to deal with something in your life. Or times when your feelings were not validated. (If not, just continue tapping on the feeling.)

Repeat one more time and then take a deep breath and measure the level of intensity in your body.

Once you are happy that the level of emotion has dropped to a 2-0 you can begin the Reframe Round.

Reframe Reclaim Round

First hold your hands over your heart.

Breathing in slowly and out slowly, see if you can create a picture in your mind of this reality and how it looks right now. How would you act differently, if you no longer felt the need to be busy all the time, and could trust your intuition? What words would you use? How would others react to you? What choices would you make? How would you choose to spend the moments in your day? Make the picture as detailed as you can.

Set-Up Statement: Even though I can sense the feeling of overwhelm dissipating, which is now a level (new level of intensity), I choose to trust and listen to my intuition and feel what it feels like, and I deeply and completely accept this new belief.

Set-Up Statement: Even though the overwhelm is no longer a strong feeling, I choose now to imagine what life would be like if I chose to live in the moment, trusting my intuition to guide me, and I deeply and completely accept this new belief in me.

Set-Up Statement: Even though there have been times in the past when I have not trusted my intuition because I was just too busy and overwhelmed, I now choose to be open to other limiting beliefs, and I choose to reclaim the beliefs that empower me, and attract opportunities into my life in many ways. And I deeply and completely accept this new belief.

EB: I choose to allow myself time to learn to trust in my intuition.

SE: I choose to release the need to be busy, and embrace living in the present moment.

UE: I choose to trust that my intuition will always guide me when I choose to listen.

UN: I choose to be open to all the possibilities that my intuition guides me towards.

CHIN: I choose to embrace this new way of being.

CB: I am now grateful for the power of my intuition and I choose to trust in my powerful inner guidance.

UA: I am so grateful for the knowledge that shows up in my life every day in many ways.

TH: I choose to embrace this way of being in all aspects of my life right now.

The Power Pose

Now stand with your hands on your hips, feet slightly apart (you can do this physically, or just imagine yourself doing it). Imagine that you are standing in the most powerful position you can. Your shoulders are back, your back is straight.

Create a powerful affirmation that resonates with you, perhaps choosing a statement from the *reframe* round.

Imagine that you are drawing up all the confidence, power, and knowledge you need through your feet and up into your heart. Then imagine that all that new energy is being distributed to every cell in your body. Hold this pose (or the image of this pose) for about 1 to 2 minutes, until you can feel this new energy powering in your body.

CHAPTER 18

Tapping to Overcome Doubt and Embrace Trust

So now you have created the intentions and started the process of clearing any blocks that may be standing in the way of your success. Now it's time to overcome doubt and embrace trust. But often that requires a huge leap of faith.

One thing I have found to be true in this co-creation process is that time is often of no relevance – or at least what we think of as time.

When you begin this process of creating intentions there are two things at play:

1. What you want may not present itself the way you think.
2. Sometimes you just have to trust!

At times the challenge to stay trusting can be extraordinary. It's a little like setting a course on your GPS – you trust it will take you to your destination, even if you ignore it a couple of times and take a different route. Eventually your GPS will re-route you and find a different way to get you to your destination.

The reason most people give up on their intentions is that they have their own self-imposed criteria. They become impatient with the process. But you may have also heard of people who gave up, just before success. Those *going to, should have, or could have* people who can tell you story after story of the dream, the idea, the opportunity that never eventuated – only to discover that somebody else created success with the very same idea!

Once you have set an intention, your job now is to stay in the present moment and focus on clearing any blocks or limiting beliefs you have around believing that the intention will be reality. If you are doing something every day to stay on track, it's time to take your hands off the steering wheel and let the plan unfold as it should.

So what happens? Well, the difference between those who persist against all odds and those who give up, all comes down to the degree of willingness to believe and trust in the process.

There have been so many times in my life where I have been pulled out of focus and flow, because I fell into fear.

Now, through tapping, I can actually *feel* the difference. I can feel when I am tipping into fear and know what I need to do when it is happening.

I will share a story of how this unfolded and how the power of staying in focus created the outcome (even though it was a scary ride).

At Christmas 2014 all our children were home for the Christmas holidays – our son and his girlfriend from Montreal; our daughter from Sydney; and our youngest daughter, who, while still living at home, was about to embark on a yearlong trip to Vancouver.

It was a special Christmas, because it was one of those, *I am not sure when this will happen again!* times.

Everything about Christmas was fabulous and fun. Then on Boxing Day night, as we had our final dinner together, we came up with a plan for all of us to meet in Vancouver in June the following year, to celebrate our son's 30th birthday.

At the time it was a bit of a pipe dream. I was using all available funds in my business to reinvest in what I needed. Gerry was working on a number of property deals, but as always in real estate the outcome, settlements, and commission payments are not in our control.

After all the kids left, Gerry and I we were sitting in the living room one night and we began talking about the trip. The question was like the elephant in the room; *how are we going to make this happen?* In order for all the kids to get to Vancouver, they would need some help from us – it was going to be an expensive exercise.

So I wrote down the things I wanted for the trip to occur:

1. We had to manifest enough money to be able to pay for all the kids while we were all together.
2. I wanted to stay in 5-star accommodation that we could afford. It had to be comfortable and conveniently located to everything we wanted to see and do.
3. I wanted to create the perfect scenario so we were able to effortlessly do everything we wanted; including catching up with friends and family we hadn't seen in over 25 years.
4. I wanted perfect weather, so that we could enjoy Canada (and not be reminded of the reason we left!).

I then wrote down all the *tail-enders* that I could think of that came up every time I thought about it.

- *It's too expensive.*
- *We can't make this happen.*
- *Nothing ever turns out the way I want.*
- *I never get what I want.*
- *Sometimes I just have to settle for second best.*

- *You can't always get what you want.*
- *Everything happens for a reason.*
- *Who are you to think you can manifest this?*
- *So many times in my life I have wanted something and it hasn't happened.*
- *What I want is just unreasonable.*
- *I am unreasonable.*
- *I don't deserve this.*

All throughout February and March I tapped every morning on the emotion behind those *tail-enders*.

As I tapped each day, different long forgotten memories were cleared. A Christmas present I wanted when I was 8 years old but I didn't get, and remembering how disappointed I was at the time because obviously Santa didn't read my letter! Missing out on gaining a position on a netball team when I was 12 years old, and feeling like my life was over! Not getting a scholarship when I was in Year 8, and feeling like I had let my parents down. Each and every memory, clearing emotion and beliefs around the times I had really wanted something and it hadn't come into my life.

February went past, March went past; I stayed focused and we told everybody we were going to Canada in June. I pulled out our suitcase and put it in our room, ready to be packed. I imagined every day what we would do, and lived as if it was just a matter of fact reality. I tapped and meditated every day, never once allowing any fear or disbelief to take over my thoughts. With each and every week the cost of the trip rose – thanks to the falling Australian dollar. But I never lost faith, and believed with my heart that it would happen. Without stress and in the most perfect way.

In April it all came together. It was my best income month of my business, and a property deal that Gerry had been working on for months settled within weeks.

That holiday we had in Canada with the kids has now been dubbed, *the best family holiday we ever had.*

Every flight transfer and connection worked perfectly (albeit a little stressful for one child who forgot to get a transit visa!). Each and every place we stayed was perfect, and beyond expectations. We only had one day of rain, and that was a day we had planned to do some shopping anyway.

What was even more wonderful was that friends we hadn't seen in 25 years were able to plan time in Vancouver the same time we were there.

It turned out to be *the holiday we couldn't have planned better if we tried!*

Were there doubts whether it would happen? Yes there were.

Were there times I wanted to just think this is all too hard? Yes there were.

Were there times when I just wanted to give up and think it was an expensive dream? Yes there were.

At so many points during the planning of that trip, I could have said *Nope this is not going to happen.* But I believed in my heart it would. I believed in my heart that it would come together *better than I thought possible.*

What made it work was clearing the limiting beliefs surrounding what I believed to be true, for me, based on past experiences and past history.

It's those voices that ring loud and true, drowning out the affirmations that you say to yourself, that create the doubt.

We are all able to manifest what we want in our lives. We can create exactly what we want in our lives by first releasing the energy around the beliefs that create the doubt.

Tapping to Overcome Doubt and Embrace Trust

For this exercise, go back and look at the intention that you set in Chapter 4.

As you are looking at the intention, measure your level of belief that this will come true, and write down any *tail-enders* that come up for you. Perhaps go back and look at the list earlier in this chapter and see if any of those statements feel true for you.

Next, try to *feel* where the emotion is in your body. Is it in your stomach? Your heart? Your head? Then measure the level of intensity on a scale of 1-10 (10 being the highest intensity) and write it down.

Let's start tapping:

Set-Up Statement: Even though I have this (intensity number) feeling that there were so many times in the past when I haven't gotten what I want, I deeply and completely accept myself and how I feel.

Set-Up Statement: Even though I have this (intensity number) feeling in my (where in your body) about never achieving what I want, and it makes me feel (emotion), I deeply and completely accept myself and how I feel.

Set-Up Statement: Even though I have this (emotion) feeling in my (where in your body) remembering all the times in my life where things never turned out the way I wanted, I deeply and completely accept myself and how I feel.

EB: This (emotion) feeling.

SE: This uncomfortable feeling.

UE: I have this disappointing feeling.

UN: This (emotion) feeling of not getting what I wanted.

CHIN: This intense feeling of (emotion) because there were so many times I missed out.

CB: This intense feeling of (emotion).

UA: Maybe I will never get what I want.

TH: This overwhelming feeling that I really want this but perhaps I will never get it.

See if you can link any patterns or memories around disappointment or sadness at not getting what you wanted in the past. (If not, just continue tapping on the feeling.)

Repeat one more time and then take a deep breath and measure the level of intensity in your body.

Once you are happy that the level of emotion has dropped to a 2-0 you can begin the Reframe Round.

Reframe Reclaim Round

Start by placing your hands on your heart, and breathing slowly.

Breathe in all the energy of patience and trust into your heart and as you breathe out release any lingering frustration or impatience.

See if you can create a picture in your mind of this new reality of trust and how it looks right now. How would you act differently, if you believed you could make your intention possible? What words would you use? What actions would you take? Who would you spend time with? How would you choose to spend the moments in your day? Your subconscious does not know the difference between what is reality now and what is yet to be reality.

Set-Up Statement: Even though I had this uncomfortable feeling, which is now a level (new level of intensity), I choose now to be comfortable and confident in trusting that this will come into my reality. And I deeply and completely accept this new belief.

Set-Up Statement: Even though the uncomfortable feeling is no longer a strong feeling, I choose now to imagine my life as if this intention was already a reality, and I deeply and completely accept this new belief in me.

Set-Up Statement: Even though I have released the intensity of disappointment in not getting what I wanted in the past, I choose to be open to other limiting beliefs, and I choose to reclaim the beliefs that empower me, and attract opportunities into my life in many ways. And I deeply and completely accept this new belief.

EB: I choose to allow myself to trust and stay in flow.

SE: I choose to release any and all self-imposed limiting beliefs about trusting myself.

UE: I choose to trust that my plan will unfold, as it should, into my life.

UN: I choose to be open to all the possibilities that will ensure my intention becomes reality.

CHIN: I choose to allow myself to begin to trust that this will be my reality.

CB: I am now grateful for this intention in my life.

UA: I am so grateful for the coincidences, ideas, and people that show up in my life every day to ensure this becomes reality.

TH: I choose to embrace this way of being in all aspects of my life right now.

The Power Pose

Now stand with your hands on your hips, feet slightly apart (you can do this physically, or just imagine yourself doing it). Imagine that you are standing in the most powerful position you can. Your shoulders are back, your back is straight.

Create a powerful affirmation that resonates with you, perhaps choosing a statement from the *reframe* round.

Imagine that you are drawing up all the confidence, power, and knowledge you need through your feet and up into your heart. Then imagine that all that new energy is being distributed to every cell in your body. Hold this pose (or the image of this pose) for about 1 to 2 minutes, until you can feel this new energy powering in your body.

CHAPTER 19

Choosing Excellence
Over Adequacy

Each and every choice we make in our lives is a reflection of what we believe about ourselves. What foods we choose to eat; what clothes we choose to wear; how we choose to spend the 1440 minutes that make up our day. Our choices reflect what we believe we are worthy of having. That belief determines what we buy, what we have – and what we put up with.

Right now stop for a moment and take a scan of the room you are in.

Are you comfortable and supported?

Does the energy in the room flow beautifully, or is it untidy and cluttered?

What food did you eat last? Was that choice made with excellence to enhance and support your energy, your body, and your health? Or was it an unconscious choice and just because it was there?

What choices have you made today that are excellent versus adequate choices? Did you get up early and exercise, meditate, tap, or journal? Did you spend time in reflection? What choice of clothing did you make? How did you spend time with your loved ones this morning?

When we make a pact with ourselves to choose excellence over adequacy, we signal to our subconscious that we are worthy of excellence. When we choose adequacy we send a message that we will accept that in our lives. It is all based around what we believe.

As you begin to honor yourself with excellence, you will begin to attract excellence in your life. You will find the perfect table at the restaurant, with the most perfect view. The perfect car park spot will suddenly appear as you drive up to it; you will see advertisements for sales of designer clothing, shoes, handbags, that you can afford. You will receive excellent service from people all around you.

The moment you choose to make excellent choices in your life, those opportunities to have excellence will show up for you.

What we believe, and what we reflect, is what we manifest in our lives. So choosing excellence comes down to whether you believe you are worthy of excellence.

But there are two important parts to choosing and allowing excellence:

1. To release your attachment to how you *expect* an outcome to show up.
2. To be grateful every day for excellence that shows up for you in the most unexpected ways − before it does.

In other words, how that excellence shows up is not expected, it is simply accepted, with gratitude.

It happens to me on a regular basis and most times without thinking. We *always* find the best table at the restaurant, arriving just as somebody else is leaving; I seem to have a heat seeking radar to discover designer clothes that are marked down well below normal retail price, usually when I am not looking!

I always seem to find the one sales person in the store who has the best customer relations, and of course my car parking angel is truly the best in the business!

It wasn't always that way, but as I began to tap regularly, I also began to understand that the beliefs that I had about myself were impacting on my choices.

I actually never really thought about the choices I made every day and how they reflected on what I believed. In particular, when it came to shopping. At the supermarket I would look for food that was convenient rather than of the best quality. When looking for clothes, I would always head straight for the sales rack, before looking elsewhere. I always looked for bargains, which is fine − I still am a bargain shopper − but it was my underlying belief about being worthy of excellence that underpinned the choices I made.

A business mentor challenged me one day to list all the areas of my life where I was accepting adequacy rather than excellence in my life. And in looking at my list she challenged me to write *I am the type of person who only buys designer clothes.*

While there was an initial feeling of excitement when I wrote those words down, when driving home I could feel the doubt creep in. *Designer labels are expensive. I can't afford designer labels.*

The next morning, I looked at my statement *I am the type of person who only buys designer clothes.* And I could feel the emotions rise. *Who are you to wear designer clothes? Who do you think you are? You are not the type of person who wears designer clothes; you will make other people feel bad. Don't think of yourself as anybody special. Just remember where you came from!*

So I began to tap on all the *tail-enders* that came up for me when I looked at the phrase. A number of them were very high on the 1-10 score and tapping helped reduce the intensity around those specific statements.

But there was one statement I could not shift, no matter how many times I tapped. *Just remember where you came from,* followed quickly by the words: *Don't rise above your station in life!*

As I tapped I remembered a conversation I had with my grandmother when I was 12 years old.

My sister and I lived with my grandparents for a few weeks as our family had come to Queensland while my father was on his long service leave. During that time, Dad wanted to evaluate the possibility of relocating our entire family from Victoria. As the time crossed over the beginning of the school year, my sister and I were enrolled in school. However, after a number of weeks of frustration, Dad was unable to find a job as good as he had at home. So they decided to return home. My sister and I stayed with my grandparents to finish the school term and would then fly home in the holidays.

My grandmother came from a family that had made money and lost money numerous times during her childhood. I remember a conversation I had with her one day after school and she was sharing a little of her story. At one stage she said, "It is important in life that you don't rise above your station." At the time I didn't quite understand what she meant, but that memory obviously had stayed with me all those years.

During one of the tapping rounds I realized I took my grandmother's words to mean that *I should always remember where I came from* and *that some people were better than me and I couldn't be friends with them.* I don't know if that is what she meant, but somehow it registered in my 12-year-old brain.

As I tapped on the memory, I could suddenly see all the times in my life where I had walked away from something because I was not to *rise above my station in life.* I specifically remember one night being asked out on a date by a medical student when I was 18 years old. I gave him the wrong number because I didn't feel I was good enough to go out with him. I remembered so many times when I didn't go to events or strike up a conversation with somebody because I didn't feel I was as good, smart, pretty, funny (whatever) as other people.

All those beliefs simply uncovered when I was challenged to *become the person who always chooses designer clothes!*

This is why tapping is so powerful. Often seemingly random thoughts or words said to us are responsible for creating beliefs that can impact on our choices throughout our lives. Tapping helps uncover and release the memories so you can make sense of how they have been affecting you. I am not sure if my grandmother actually meant those words, or even realized the impact they had on me, but in my 12-year-old mind, they went in and stayed there. It doesn't make my grandmother right or wrong, it is simply how I interpreted her words.

It is never about what happens or what is said to you – rather it is the impact of the event or the words that holds the influence over you. That is why what we say to our children is *so* important. The imaginative child brain takes words literally and creates a reaction to those words. The child then forms opinions about themselves and life that dictates their future.

So I tapped and reduced the intensity to the memory of the words my grandmother said to me. Then I reframed my belief to *I choose to believe I am the type of person who always wears designer clothes.* I continued to tap on that statement for a few more days. Being very mindful of any *tail-enders,* that popped into my mind, until there was simply no more charge on the words.

As if by magic, suddenly opportunities to buy designer outfits at reasonable prices appeared in my life.

Two days after clearing the belief, I attended a networking event and there was an exhibitor who had clothes imported from the US. I saw a purple outfit, so I reached in and pulled it off the rack – it was a Ralph Lauren dress, my perfect size and only $50!

A week later I was in Melbourne with my daughter. We walked by a thrift store and for some reason I felt compelled to walk in. On the rack was a gorgeous Anne Klein dress and jacket in my size for $39!

Four weeks later, I was at a large department store that happened to be holding a 30% off sale. I wasn't really focused on buying anything, but as I walked past one of the racks I saw a gorgeous designer top in my size. The original price was $185; it had been marked down by 50% already, then a further 30% for the sale. So I tried it on – and it was perfect! When I got to the register to pay for it the sales girl said, "Oh that's a green label; there is a further 50% off those today." So the $185 designer top was reduced to the princely sum of $29 just for me! I didn't stop smiling the whole way home.

I am never sure which thing I am more excited about – finding a designer outfit I love, or getting it on a massive sale!

Suddenly everywhere I looked there were opportunities to choose excellence. As I changed my limiting belief around, *I am the person who wears designer clothing*, my focus shifted to be aware of opportunities that supported my new belief. Were those opportunities always there? Probably! Were there other opportunities prior to clearing the belief that I didn't see? More than likely.

But my attention shifted. My intuition became heightened and aware of opportunities to allow me to experience that new belief. It's the phenomena of *Frequency of Illusion* and *Confirmation Bias* going into overdrive!

The minute you shift a limiting belief, all manner of opportunities begin to appear to fulfill what you now believe.

When living in the state of acceptance and gratitude *and* without the attachment to outcome, life begins to flow easily and joyfully. It's a fabulous thing!

Tapping on Choosing Excellence Over Adequate

For this exercise, go back and look at the intention you set in Chapter 4, and ask yourself these questions: "Where in my life do I choose adequate over excellence?" "Where in the past did I believe I was not worthy of excellence in my life?" "What choices would I have to make now in order to attract more excellence in my life?"

Next, try to *feel* if there is any emotion surrounding choosing excellence? Is it an uncomfortable feeling in your stomach? Your heart? Your head? Then measure the level of intensity on a scale of 1-10 (10 being the highest intensity) and write it down.

Let's start tapping:

Set-Up Statement: Even though I have this (intensity number) feeling because I am not sure I deserve excellence in my life, I deeply and completely accept myself and how I feel.

Set-Up Statement: Even though I have this (intensity number) feeling in my (where in your body) about not feeling worthy to have excellence in all my choices, and it makes me feel (emotion), I deeply and completely accept myself and how I feel.

Set-Up Statement: Even though I have this (emotion) feeling in my (where in your body) whenever I think about attracting excellence in my life, I deeply and completely accept myself and how I feel.

EB: This (emotion) feeling.

SE: This uncomfortable feeling.

UE: I have never felt I deserved excellence in my life.

UN: This (emotion) feeling of not feeling worthy to have excellence in my life.

CHIN: This intense feeling of (emotion) because I feel this hesitation around the choices I have made in the past.

CB: This intense feeling of (emotion).

UA: I don't feel worthy or deserving of excellence.

TH: This overwhelming feeling of unworthiness to have excellence in my life.

See if you can link any patterns or memories around not feeling worthy or deserving of excellence. (If not, just continue tapping on the feeling.)

Repeat one more time and then take a deep breath and measure the level of intensity in your body.

Once you are happy that the level of emotion has dropped to a 2-0 you can begin the Reframe Round.

Reframe Reclaim Round

Place your hands over your heart, and breathe slowly and deeply. Imagine if whatever you want to create, is in your life right now. That every choice, every action, and every word you use reflects your new belief of being deserving of excellence. You are rewiring your beliefs, thoughts, and your actions to reflect what you want in your life. That includes acting as if it is already here!

Set-Up Statement: Even though I had this uncomfortable feeling, which is now a level (new level of intensity), I choose now to accept excellence in my life always. And I deeply and completely accept this new belief.

Set-Up Statement: Even though the uncomfortable feeling is no longer a strong feeling, I choose now to imagine what life would be like if I believed I was worthy of excellence, and I deeply and completely accept this new belief in me.

Set-Up Statement: Even though I have released the intensity of feeling unworthy of excellence, I choose to be open to other limiting beliefs, and I choose to reclaim the beliefs that empower me, and attract opportunities into my life in many ways. And I deeply and completely accept this new belief.

EB: I choose to allow myself time to be open to the excellent opportunities that arise for me.

SE: I choose to release any and all self-imposed limiting beliefs around excellence.

UE: I choose to allow all manner of excellence to flow into my life in many ways.

UN: I choose to be open to all the possibilities and release my attachment to the outcome.

CHIN: I choose for excellence to flow into my life in perfect ways.

CB: I am now grateful for all excellence that flows through me and my life.

UA: I am so grateful for the excellence that shows up in my life every day in many ways.

TH: I choose to embrace this way of excellence in all aspects of my life right now.

The Power Pose

Now stand with your hands on your hips, feet slightly apart (you can do this physically, or just imagine yourself doing it). Imagine that you are standing in the most powerful position you can. Your shoulders are back, your back is straight.

Create a powerful affirmation that resonates with you, perhaps choosing a statement from the *reframe* round.

Imagine that you are drawing up all the confidence, power, and knowledge you need through your feet and up into your heart. Then imagine that all that new energy is being distributed to every cell in your body. Hold this pose (or the image of this pose) for about 1 to 2 minutes, until you can feel this new energy powering in your body.

CHAPTER 20

Tapping to Release the Need to be Perfect

It was late on the second day of my two-day event, where I challenge my clients to look at all areas of their lives where they are accepting adequacy instead of excellence. One of the participants, Julie, asked, "But how is excellence different from perfection? I am struggling to overcome my need for perfectionism in my life; isn't this the same?"

I explained it to her this way. Perfection is a way of controlling what we can in our lives when our life feels out of control. Striving for perfection indicates that you believe something about you, your life, and those around you is imperfect. You no longer trust in the co-creation process; instead, you feel alone and isolated. Perfectionism often camouflages the feeling that life is too scary and you can only create peace by creating order.

Excellence is when we believe ourselves to be worthy of all that supports us. Excellence in the foods we choose, the clothes we wear, and the people we choose to spend our valuable time with.

211

By choosing excellence in our lives, we send a signal to our subconscious that we are worthy of excellence.

The key is to release any beliefs blocking the flow of excellence in our lives. To express gratitude before it appears and release the attachment to the outcome of how it appears. When this happens, we move to the perfect place of co-creation with our *Higher Self.*

Perfection is about control and fear. Excellence is about choice and trust.

Julie was still looking at me and I could see tears welling up in her eyes. I asked her if she wanted to tap on the emotion and see if we could make some sense of it.

Julie's Story

Julie is a recovering perfectionist. Prior to tapping on her need for perfection, Julie drove herself (and everybody else) crazy with her need to have everything perfect. Her house was immaculate, her car was always as clean as if it had been just driven off the lot, and even her walk-in wardrobe was color coordinated with matching coat hangers!

I asked what her trigger was when we talked about excellence versus adequacy. She said, "I have struggled with perfectionism all my life; I still struggle with it now. I am feeling really uncomfortable with choosing excellence; I don't understand the difference."

I asked her to tell me how she felt right now, and she could feel a sense of panic and high anxiety in her chest. So we tapped first to bring the levels of anxiety and panic down. Then I asked her about the feelings she felt when I asked her to choose excellence.

"You know, I was one of these people who had to have everything right, even back in my school days. Everything had to be perfect. I would do school work over and over again, just because I didn't think the writing in my book was perfect enough. I would re-iron my school uniform because I didn't think my mother did it properly.

I would get up in the morning and make my bed and clean my room – every morning!"

I asked Julie if there was a time in her life where she felt that if she was perfect, things would be better.

She looked at me and said, "My mother and father used to have the most awful arguments about money. I don't know why, but I can remember my mother throwing something at him one night; I must have been about 8 years old."

So I asked Julie to recall the incident while she tapped.

She remembered feeling so frightened and worried about her parents. So we tapped on all the feelings that she recalled. Then suddenly she said, "I just remembered what it was. I remember Mum throwing a vase at Dad one night and the glass shattered everywhere. My brother and I were hiding in the bedroom. I made him stay there and I went out and started to sweep up the shattered glass. My Dad and Mum stopped arguing and were just looking at me while I cleaned the glass up. Mum thanked me and gave me a hug!"

I asked her if she could recall how she felt when that happened. She said, "I felt in control of the situation; I can almost feel myself saying to myself, 'I've got this. I can do this! If I am perfect I can stop you guys from arguing.'"

Then she said, "I just got it; if I am perfect, I get love. Just by making things perfect again, I can control everything. Even when things feel scary and out of control!"

Perfectionism stems from a desire to be in control. For many people, while their world or lives may be spinning out of control, if they can control their external environment by insisting on perfection, whether that be in their body, their work, or house – it feels as if one aspect is in control.

In Julie's case, by cleaning up the broken vase, she made her parents stop arguing for a moment and she felt she could control an out-of-control environment.

On the last call of the program, Julie said, "Sally, you would be so proud of me, I actually went to bed last night and left some dirty dishes in the sink! I didn't even notice till I got up this morning. Wow, I feel so much more relaxed about life. I really love this new me!"

By tapping Julie has been able to release the emotion around the need for perfectionism and control. While Julie is still a person who likes order in her life, now she feels she is not driven by the need to have everything perfect all the time.

Tapping on the Need to be Perfect and in Control

For this exercise, check on any places in your life where you feel the need to be in control or be perfect?

How does that emotion feel in your body?

Is it fear? Is it frustration? Is it anxiety? Is it sadness? Is it a sense of *if I can't control this something bad might happen?*

Next, try to *feel* where the emotion is in your body. Is it in your stomach? Your heart? Your head? Then measure the level of intensity on a scale of 1-10 (10 being the highest intensity) and write it down.

Let's start tapping:
Set-Up Statement: Even though I have this (intensity number) feeling because I have this need to have perfection in my life, I deeply and completely accept myself and how I feel.

Set-Up Statement: Even though I have this (intensity number) feeling in my (where in your body) about being scared if my life is out of control, and it makes me feel (emotion), I deeply and completely accept myself and how I feel.

Set-Up Statement: Even though I have this (emotion) feeling in my (where in your body) whenever I think about the need to have perfection in my life, I deeply and completely accept myself and how I feel.

EB: This (emotion) feeling.
SE: This uncomfortable feeling.
UE: This perfectionism.
UN: This (level of intensity) feeling of fear around not being in control.
CHIN: This intense feeling of (emotion) because everything has to be perfect.
CB: This intense feeling of (emotion).
UA: I just am not sure what would happen if things were not perfect.
TH: This overwhelming feeling of the need to be in control.

See if you can link any patterns or memories around feeling out of control or feeling that if life was perfect you would be in control. (If not, just continue tapping on the feeling.)

Repeat one more time and then take a deep breath and measure the level of intensity in your body.

Once you are happy that the level of emotion has dropped to a 2-0 you can begin the Reframe Round.

Reframe Reclaim Round

Place your hands over your heart, and breathe slowly and deeply. Imagine you are breathing energy into your heart, and as you breath out releasing the energy that no longer serves you.

Now, imagine what it would feel like to release your need for perfectionism. What would that be like? What difference would that make in your life? What difference would that make to others? How would you act differently?

Set-Up Statement: Even though I had this uncomfortable feeling, which is now a level (new level of intensity), I choose now to imagine what life would be like if I didn't feel the need to be perfect. And I deeply and completely accept this new belief.

Set-Up Statement: Even though the uncomfortable feeling is no longer a strong feeling, I choose now to imagine what life would be like for me if I chose to trust and release the need to be in control, and I deeply and completely accept this new belief in me.

Set-Up Statement: Even though I have released the intensity of things in my life needing to be perfect, I choose to be open to other limiting beliefs, and I choose to reclaim the beliefs that empower me, and attract opportunities into my life in many ways. And I deeply and completely accept this new belief.

EB: I choose to allow myself time to release the need to be perfect.
SE: I choose to release any and all self-imposed limiting beliefs about me.
UE: I choose to allow the feeling of unlimited love and trust to flow easily into my life.
UN: I choose to be open to all the possibilities of allowing excellence, without the need to control the outcome.
CHIN: I choose to allow my truest self to feel safe and secure.
CB: I am now grateful for all the ways in which I am supported and loved in my life.
UA: I am so grateful for the love and support that shows up in my life every day in many ways.
TH: I choose to embrace this way of being in all aspects of my life right now.

The Power Pose

Now stand with your hands on your hips, feet slightly apart (you can do this physically, or just imagine yourself doing it). Imagine that you are standing in the most powerful position you can. Your shoulders are back, your back is straight.

Create a powerful affirmation that resonates with you, perhaps choosing a statement from the *reframe* round.

Imagine that you are drawing up all the confidence, power, and knowledge you need through your feet and up into your heart. Then imagine that all that new energy is being distributed to every cell in your body. Hold this pose (or the image of this pose) for about 1 to 2 minutes, until you can feel this new energy powering in your body.

CHAPTER 21

Tapping to Overcome Feelings of Shame or Regret

As we continue to release emotion and move into flow to manifest what we want, often the most difficult emotions to release are deep feelings of shame or regret. Mostly brought about by failures from the past.

Personally, I don't buy into the phrase *I have no regrets*; I don't believe that to be true. I think if you are a living, loving, warm-hearted human, there are times in your life when you have regretted some of the choices that you have made − and that's okay. It's what makes us human.

We claim back our infinite power when we unpack and understand the emotional space we were in at the time we made that decision. The key is to forgive ourselves for all those decisions we didn't make; the calls we didn't take; the words we didn't say; or the love we didn't express.

Whenever we say something in anger, make a decision that is not in our best interest, or pretend that we are okay with something when clearly we are not – it simply means we are operating from a place of our shattered selves.

Every time we are hurt, or when words cut through our hearts like a knife, or when our world feels painful and dark, it's as if small pieces of us are splintered and shattered. We struggle to remember who we really are and sometimes we can say or do things that we regret.

The feelings of shame or embarrassment that come from those regrets hold us back from truly reclaiming the whole of us. But when we are able to release and forgive the regrets, we free ourselves to begin to express from the wholeness of us. We gather up the shattered pieces and we reclaim our real self.

We are not our patterns. We are not even our emotions, but it is our patterns and our emotions that can dominate our lives and dictate our responses.

When our emotions are out of control, it simply means we have, for a moment, become overwhelmed.

By understanding, releasing, and forgiving those emotions of regret, shame, or embarrassment, we are free to create a new path. This is when we can attract what we want in our lives without the feeling that we might *screw up* again.

Annie's Story

Annie had been a teacher for most of her life but after 25 years, she wanted to try something else. She was a born talker, so friends had suggested that she might like being in real estate. She took a year off teaching, got her real estate license, and used the time to see if she could help people buy and sell their homes.

Initially, she really loved the idea of selling houses. She enjoyed holding open homes, chatting, and getting to know people. She soon found that she didn't really need to *sell* anything.

She just talked to people and found out what they loved and prided herself on creating a great match.

But she started to find that the *selling* of real estate was different from *talking* about it. For the first six months or so, most of her clients were people who either knew her or had been recommended to her by others.

Eventually, those leads began to dry up and she found herself having to work to get listings and even harder to get sales. All of a sudden she dreaded getting up in the morning and the days dragged on. She began to worry that perhaps she wasn't very good at this sales thing, but the thought of returning to teaching didn't feel right either. She felt stuck.

I asked Annie to tell me a bit of her story; in particular, any memories she had around money.

She came from a loving family, the eldest of five kids. Her mother and father were hard workers who saved well for their retirement and once the kids were all off their hands, they began to travel.

When Annie and her husband bought their first house, her parents helped them out with the initial down payment on the house. Interest rates at the time were high, but Annie and her husband made enough money to cover the mortgage repayments.

Their plan was to pay off as much of the house as possible before they settled down to become parents. The problem was that their first baby didn't take any notice of their plan, and Annie fell pregnant two years earlier than expected.

To top it all off, her husband was retrenched from his high paying job and could only find casual work. He fell into depression as he struggled to find work, putting an increased strain on their relationship.

They began to fall further and further behind in their mortgage payments. One night in tears, Annie phoned her father to ask if he could lend them $10,000 to get them through the next six months. Her dad agreed, but within months they were behind again –

and to make it worse, Annie was pregnant again. She had to ask her dad to help them out again.

I asked her to explain the emotions she felt asking her dad for money

"I felt ashamed and embarrassed actually. Here we were, two well-educated people who couldn't afford to pay our mortgage and had to ask my parents for help. I just felt that if I was so good, why did I have to ask for money?"

So we tapped on the phrase: *If I was so good why do I have to ask for money,* and the feelings of shame and embarrassment she felt in having to resort to asking her parents for help.

As we continued to tap to get the intensity of the feelings down, I noticed her face change and her eyes move from side to side.

I asked her what happened. She said, "You know, I was doing okay selling real estate when I actually didn't have to do the selling or ask for money. The people who bought those houses in the initial stages were friends or friends of friends. They came to me because they wanted me to facilitate the process! Now, I actually have to ask people for the sale and for the money. If I am so good, why do I have to ask for the money?"

"Oh my god," she said. "That's it, I feel ashamed and embarrassed to ask people for money because when I had to ask my Dad for money I really felt so ashamed. Wow, I can actually feel that feeling lighten up in my stomach. I have been carrying that feeling for years. I can remember so many times in these last few months where I had the same feeling when it came to closing a sale. I felt embarrassed to ask and I couldn't figure it out!"

The shame, embarrassment, and regret of past errors are emotions that sit deep in our mind. A place we don't want to go to because it feels too painful or too dark. But they don't define us; they are a result of us at some point feeling alone, frightened, unloved, unaccepted, or unwanted.

They are not you. They represent a time in your life where you were not the whole of you. Where circumstances, events, people, or words caused you pain and in that space and time, you responded the best way you knew how.

Now it's time to forgive and release those feelings and emotions because they no longer serve you. It's like a little annoying person who sits on your shoulder all the time telling you all the reasons why you are a bad person who doesn't deserve to get what you want. But those emotions and feelings serve no purpose; they impact on your confidence and belief in yourself and hold you back from trusting your innate powerful wisdom and intuition.

Tapping on Releasing Shame and Regret

For this tapping exercise, write a list of the times in your life that you feel embarrassed, ashamed, or regretful. For this particular exercise, there may be a number of times that have that little *twinge* of feeling when you recall them. See if you can pick one or two that have the most uncomfortable feeling and put the level of intensity next to it. Next, measure where you can feel that in your body, and see if you can get as specific as you can about how it feels and where the feeling sits.

Then measure the level of intensity on a scale of 1-10 (10 being the highest intensity) and write it down.

Let's start tapping:
Set-Up Statement: Even though I have this (intensity number) feeling because I feel all this regret about this time in my life, I deeply and completely accept myself and how I feel.

Set-Up Statement: Even though I have this (intensity number) feeling in my (where in your body) and it makes me feel (emotion), I deeply and completely accept myself and how I feel.

Set-Up Statement: Even though I have this (emotion) feeling in my (where in your body) whenever I think about that time, I deeply and completely accept myself and how I feel.

EB: This (emotion) feeling.
SE: These feelings of (emotion).
UE: This (level of intensity) (emotion).
UN: This (emotion) feeling.
CHIN: This intense feeling of (emotion) when I think of that time.
CB: This intense feeling of (emotion).
UA: I feel so (emotion) when I think of that time, I wish I could change it.
TH: This overwhelming feeling of (emotion).

See if you can link any patterns or other memories around the feeling of embarrassment, shame, or regret. (If not, just continue tapping on the feeling.)

Repeat one more time and then take a deep breath and measure the level of intensity in your body.

Once you are happy that the level of emotion has dropped to a 2-0 you can begin the Reframe Round.

Reframe Reclaim Round

Place your hands over your heart, and breathe slowly and deeply. Imagine you are breathing energy into your heart, and as you breath out releasing the energy that no longer serves you.

Imagine whatever you want to create, is in your life right now. What does it feel like to feel as if you have forgiven yourself for those times when you felt regretful? That every choice, every action, and every word you use reflects your new belief of releasing and forgiving any feelings of shame or regret. You are rewiring your beliefs, thoughts, and your actions to reflect what you want in your life. That includes acting as if it is already here!

Set-Up Statement: Even though I had this uncomfortable feeling, which is now a level (new level of intensity), I choose now forgive myself for what happened. And I deeply and completely accept this new belief.

Set-Up Statement: Even though the (emotion) feeling is no longer a strong feeling, I choose now to imagine what life would be like if I chose to forgive myself for that time, and I deeply and completely accept this new belief in me.

Set-Up Statement: Even though I have released the intensity of this (feeling), I choose to be open to other limiting beliefs, and I choose to reclaim the beliefs that empower me, and attract opportunities into my life in many ways. And I deeply and completely accept this new belief.

EB: I choose to forgive myself and release these feelings of regret.
SE: I choose to release any and all self-imposed limiting beliefs that stem from that time.
UE: I choose to allow forgiveness and love for myself to flow easily into my life.
UN: I choose to accept that I made that decision at a time when I was (emotion).

CHIN: I choose to release the feelings of shame and regret as they no longer serve the *who* I am now.

CB: I am now grateful for the love and forgiveness that I feel flowing through my body.

UA: I am so grateful for the love and compassion that shows up in my life every day in many ways.

TH: I choose to embrace this way of being in my life every day right now.

The Power Pose

Now stand with your hands on your hips, feet slightly apart (you can do this physically, or just imagine yourself doing it). Imagine that you are standing in the most powerful position you can. Your shoulders are back, your back is straight.

Create a powerful affirmation that resonates with you, perhaps choosing a statement from the *reframe* round.

Imagine that you are drawing up all the confidence, power, and knowledge you need through your feet and up into your heart. Then imagine that all that new energy is being distributed to every cell in your body. Hold this pose (or the image of this pose) for about 1 to 2 minutes, until you can feel this new energy powering in your body.

CHAPTER 22

When Criticism Sometimes Equals Love

Moira was one of the first clients in my eight-week *Reclaim You* program. She was struggling with losing weight and felt low in energy most days.

She had a whole closet of *fat clothes* and *thin clothes* and she was a habitual *yo-yo* dieter. She would diet and exercise to lose the weight, feel great, but after a while, she would put it all back on again. Nothing she tried seemed to work in the long run.

Even though her weight was frustrating her, there was another issue that was causing her stress. Her manager in her workplace was becoming increasingly difficult to work with. Moira felt undermined and dismissed whenever she was around her. No matter what she did or how hard she worked, this manager seemed to find fault in the smallest things. Going to work each day was becoming exceptionally stressful and she felt like she just wanted to leave.

Moira's Story

In our first session together, I asked Moira what level she felt her stress levels were. Immediately she said a level 8, especially when she thought of work. She felt her energy levels at a level 3, finding her usual high energy abandoning her.

Over the course of the program, we started seeing results. Moira would use tapping at work to lower her stress levels and as she did so, her energy levels increased. She was able to resume exercising in the morning because she needed less sleep, but her weight was still not shifting. She felt that there was an underlying limiting belief that was stopping her from losing weight. Although we had tapped on many issues – there was still something she felt was causing her to sabotage her eating behaviors and the frustration with her manager.

Halfway through the program, we finally got to both the issue with her weight and the challenges with her manager. And both were linked to a memory from her childhood.

Moira had grown up in a family where her father was very dominant. The eldest of three children, Moira felt it was her responsibility to be the successful one in the family. She was a talented sportsperson and often won many awards for her sporting ability.

However, it didn't seem to matter how much she achieved or how many awards she won, her father never acknowledged her success. Instead, he constantly criticized her. He didn't believe in praising children. Rather, he always told her that no matter how good you are, there was always room for improvement.

As an adult, Moira could justify her father's action was his way of motivating her to strive for further success. However, I asked Moira to describe how it felt to her as a child. She recalled feeling as if nothing she ever did was good enough. That no matter how hard she tried, he never told her he was proud of her or that he loved her.

I asked her to recall the first time she could remember the pain of criticism from her father. Her first memory was as an 8-year-old child when she had won the *most improved* award for her team. We tapped as she recalled running up to her dad to show him the trophy. She then recalled the hurt feeling when he told her that she should have won the *best player* award because she was better than that. She saw her 8-year-old self, standing in front of her dad, feeling sad, hurt, and disappointed in her heart. She was also shocked to recall a memory from that time where she believed that if she was just the best at everything, one day he would have to say he loved her.

As we tapped on the sadness of never receiving praise from her father, Moira she could see how her whole life she was striving for praise and reassurance. No matter what she did, she was always looking for somebody to praise her and when it didn't come, she just tried harder.

In that moment, Moira suddenly linked her weight issues to the same belief. "Whenever I lose weight I feel good for a few weeks because I get so many compliments from people. But the minute the compliments stop, I feel like nobody notices me. I put all the weight back on, then I lose it again; it just goes around and around in a circle. In fact, last week I thought, wow it's like nobody is noticing me! There it is right there – that's why I sabotage myself – all the time!"

As we continued to tap on the need for reassurance and acknowledgement from others, she realized how the issue with her manager was connected. She was constantly seeking praise from her manager. In doing so, she was almost seeking out the criticism as a way of being validated in the job so at least her boss would notice her. "I get it," she said, "I have attracted somebody in my life just like my Dad! If she criticizes me, at least she notices me. Good grief, it's all backwards."

As the tears stopped and the intensity released, Moira's entire body seemed to glow and actually look lighter. She connected the pattern.

Her father's way of showing love was to give what he thought was constructive feedback, but she only saw it as criticism. It became the way she felt *seen and loved* by her father. And while it was not what she wanted – it was what she knew. That was the pattern she kept attracting into her life.

By the time the program finished, Moira had lost 5kg. The relationship with her boss had improved so much so that her boss often popped into her office offering her coffee!

Moira's story is an example of how we continue to recreate the patterns of our lives. Like a mirror, we attract what we accept as truth for us. Our vibrational energy is like a heat seeking missile. It keeps creating the same pattern in your life until you are ready to clear it. But it is just a pattern. Once you recognize the cause of the pattern it is easy to release it, by understanding the belief that created it in the first place.

When we feel loved we also feel connected, powerful, and confident to be *who* we truly are. As we *reclaim* our truest self, many times it involves finding and understanding a time when love wasn't present in the past – and rediscovering *what* or *who* was put into place to substitute the pain of the emptiness of love.

Reclaiming You is the process of releasing the pain of *no love*. To forgive the person or event that made you feel that way. Then to heal the years of lack of love and the confusion which played itself out in the choices that you made. From there, replacing the lack of love with a love of self.

Once that happens, the opportunities to manifest success will swing into place. But it first begins with understanding and healing that part of you that felt that first twinge of pain. When you first realized that the world was not a place of joy and love, but could be a place of disappointment, loneliness, isolation, and pain. And to heal the confusion and the sadness that created the patterns that keep playing themselves out in your present reality.

Tapping to Rediscover Love of You

For this exercise, I would like you to be mindful of any area of your life where there is a pattern where you are replacing love of self with something else. Whether that be food, alcohol, your relationships, habits that do not enhance you, or the words that you use to describe yourself.

Try to *feel* what that emotion is and where the emotion is in your body, and what level of intensity you believe it to be true. Write down both.

Let's start tapping:

Set-Up Statement: Even though I can see how I have created this pattern in my life, I deeply and completely accept myself and how I feel.

Set-Up Statement: Even though there were so many times in my life when I felt as if who I was just wasn't good enough and it makes me feel (emotion), I deeply and completely accept myself and how I feel.

Set-Up Statement: Even though sometimes I recreate this same pattern of (emotion), I deeply and completely accept myself and how I feel.

EB: This pattern of (emotion/feeling).
SE: There were so many times that I made choices because I felt I wasn't good enough.
UE: My (parent) could not express love.

UN: There were very few times in my life when I felt loved for who I was.

CHIN: This sadness at always feeling (emotion/feeling).

CB: So many choices I made in my life because I was just looking to feel loved.

UA: I struggle to feel love for me.

TH: So many times I did things because I just wanted to be loved.

Repeat one more time and then take a deep breath and measure the level of intensity in your body.

See if you can link any patterns or memories of your life to the feeling of not being loved.

Once you are happy that the level feels like a 2-0 you can begin the Reframe Round.

Reframe Reclaim Round

Start by placing your hands on your heart, and breathing slowly. Breathe in all the energy of love into your heart, and as you breathe out release any energy that no longer serves you.

Remember now to imagine as if you are totally loved. Feel what that love feels like as you breathe deeply and allow that feeling of love to flow from your heart to every cell of your body.

See if you can create a picture in your mind of this reality and how it looks right now. How would you act differently, if this was already in your life? What words would you use? What actions would you take? Who would you spend time with? How would you choose to spend the moments in your day?

Set-Up Statement: Even though I have this memory of not feeling loved, which is now a (level of intensity), I choose now to forgive (parent) for not being there when I needed love. And I deeply and completely accept this new belief.

231

Set-Up Statement: Even though this lack of love has stopped me from achieving intentions in the past, I now choose to forgive (parent) so I can be free. And I deeply and completely accept this new belief in me.

Set-Up Statement: Even though I feel I have released much of the hurt, I choose now to be open to other limiting beliefs that may still be present so I can clear them and I choose to reclaim the beliefs that empower me, and attract opportunities into my life in many ways. And I deeply and completely accept this new belief.

EB: I choose to allow myself to forgive (parent) for their inability to express love.

SE: I choose to release any and all self-imposed limiting beliefs that stemmed from the times when I felt that there was nobody to love me.

UE: I choose to feel love for myself and others.

UN: I choose to allow forgiveness to be a part of every day of my life.

CHIN: I choose to forgive so I can be free to be me.

CB: I feel grateful for this power of forgiveness and open my heart to attract love into my life each and every day.

UA: I am so grateful for the opportunity to show love in my life every day in many ways.

TH: I choose to embrace this new feeling of love in my life in many ways, every day.

The Power Pose

Now stand with your hands on your hips, feet slightly apart (you can do this physically, or just imagine yourself doing it). Imagine that you are standing in the most powerful position you can. Your shoulders are back, your back is straight.

Create a powerful affirmation that resonates with you, perhaps choosing a statement from the *reframe* round.

Imagine that you are drawing up all the confidence, power, love, and forgiveness you need through your feet and up into your heart. Then imagine that all that new energy is being distributed to every cell in your body. Hold this pose (or the image of this pose) for about 1 to 2 minutes, until you can feel this new energy powering in your body.

CHAPTER 23

Why Affirmations Don't Work and How Tapping Can Help

Many people I know are great believers in saying affirmations. Phrases such as: *I attract large sums of money into my life,* or *My body is my perfect weight,* or *Success comes to me in many ways.*

While saying affirmations can be powerful, they won't make any difference in your reality if what you believe about yourself is not in alignment with the words you say!

For instance, when I speak at events about money, I always ask two questions:

1. "Who here says affirmations about money that go something like: "Money comes to me easily and abundantly?" or "My bank account is overflowing with money flowing to me in many ways?"

    Usually, almost 75% of participants would put up their hands. Then I ask:

2. "So how's that working for you?"

The biggest response? "Not at all!"

I have had many clients say, "You know, I do all the right things. I think positively, I have affirmations written everywhere – so how come I am always struggling?"

The answer is not in the words you use, but what you believe is true for you.

Saying affirmations and thinking positively won't work unless your beliefs are in alignment. Otherwise it's like putting a Band-Aid on a wound, without cleaning the wound first. Unless you clean out any possible cause for infection, the wound will not heal effectively.

Tapping helps do that by clearing out the negative beliefs that are holding you back from creating success.

From there, setting powerful affirmations becomes easy. Because you are not fighting with beliefs that are incongruent with what you want.

The moment we set an intention to achieve something, two things happen:

1. The process of bringing that intention to fruition begins.
2. Quickly followed by every limiting belief you have ever had in your life suddenly moving into action!

Those *tail-enders,* often affectionately referred to as the *Itty Bitty Shitty Committee* that lives in your head, come alive and very noisy. It is the power of those *tail-enders* that bring intentions to a grinding halt, creating blocks, excuses, procrastination, and disbelief in your world.

Donna's Story

Donna considered herself a pioneer in the *positive thinking* movement. As a young girl she was fascinated by anything to do with reincarnation, alternative therapies, self-development, affirmations, and positive thinking. She had a list of affirmations she used regularly, but lately she was feeling as if they were not working.

She was married and had her two daughters when she was in her very early 20s. She and her husband divorced some 20 years later and by the time she was 50, both her girls had left home, gone to university, and one daughter had provided her with twin grandchildren. At first, she wasn't thrilled to be a grandmother at the ripe old age of 50, but she truly loved the twins.

She had worked as a successful graphic artist and lived in a large regional area before her daughter suffered a serious health condition. During treatment, Donna moved in to help her son-in-law care for the children.

After her daughter was given the all clear, Donna felt as if she needed to stay close to her daughter and family, so she bought a small townhouse nearby. While she tried to acclimatize to her new surroundings, she felt lost and disconnected.

None of her former spiritual and affirmation practices seemed to work. She was having trouble attracting clients, and the ones she did were often hard to deal with. She felt her creativity being challenged and while she had plenty of savings to draw on, it was the types of clients she was attracting that were causing her to go through a period of self-doubt and lack of confidence.

"I say affirmations every day. I focus on thinking positively. What the heck? I am struggling to attract clients, which has never been an issue for me, and either the clients I do attract are so difficult, or I am chasing them for money. I have never had this problem before when I lived in the country."

I asked Donna to first tell me what her ideal client was like. What did they look like? What industry were they in? Age, location, income, etc.

From there we did a mind map of any negative thoughts or feelings that came up for her when she imagined her perfect client.

She struggled for a while and then said, "But if I say the negative, won't I attract that?"

I explained that this was the process of first honoring her thoughts and then reducing the amount of emotional intensity she had around them. The more you try and ignore the negative thoughts, the stronger they become. It's as if they create some type of invisible energy field around you, stopping the good stuff from getting to you!

So with a deep breath she suddenly allowed every negative thought she ever had to flow!

- *I am not good enough to work in the city.*
- *I am only a country girl at heart.*
- *Who would listen to me?*
- *What if they found out that I don't have a degree?*
- *I am 50, maybe I am too old.*
- *What if I can't keep up with the intensity in the city?*
- *What if people find out I am a grandmother – will they treat me like an old lady?*
- *What if I am running out of energy?*
- *What if I start forgetting things?*
- *I don't feel I belong here.*
- *They take advantage of country people in the city you know.*
- *You can't trust city people.*

The list went on for about 20 more lines.

When she had finished writing, she just sat there for a moment and finally said, "Wow, I just feel so much lighter just getting those out of my head!"

So, listening a little to my intuition, I asked her about the statements: *You can't trust city people; they take advantage of country people you know.* I then asked her where that phrase came from.

"My Dad," she said. "He used to say that all the time. We grew up in a small country town where everybody knew each other. We all used to leave our doors unlocked. It was the type of town where every person knew who you were, and you called all the adults *auntie* or *uncle.* But one year, I think I was about eight years old, there was a series of break-ins at various businesses in town, including my Dad's store. People became very suspicious and started locking their doors at night. As kids we had to be home before dark, where previously we could roam as much as we liked. They found out later that the robberies were carried out by two itinerant workers who had come from the city to help with fruit picking."

So I asked her to say the belief out loud and measure on a scale of 1-10 how strong the truth of that was for her. She remembered feeling scared during that time, like suddenly the innocence of her country life disappeared. She actually recalled it was the first time she felt scared of anybody, especially unknown people from the city. Surprising to her – it felt like a level 8, and she felt it in her stomach. So we tapped until the intensity came down and she said, "You know, that is a sentence I just say all the time, just as a joke really – and I didn't even realize how much of a belief it really was. That is amazing!"

Donna phoned me two weeks later to say that all of a sudden she was starting to get calls from great clients who were a pleasure to work with, and one client who she was chasing for money unexpectedly paid her.

Tapping When Affirmations Don't Work

For this exercise, write a list of affirmations you always say, whether it is about money, success, weight, or attracting a relationship.

At each affirmation, stop and just see if there are any negative or limiting beliefs.

For instance:

Affirmation	What you really believe!
Money comes to me in many ways	*No it doesn't.* *For everybody else but me.* *I always have to struggle for money.*
I am my perfect weight	*As if!* *Everything I eat ends up on my hips anyway!* *Losing weight is too hard.*
I attract my perfect partner	*All the good men are gone!* *All men are idiots.* *I am like a beacon for the man I can't have.*

Now measure the *feeling in your body* when you look at those affirmations and *tail-enders*.

Next, try to *feel* where the emotion is in your body. Is it in your stomach? Your heart? Your head? Then measure the level of intensity on a scale of 1-10 (10 being the highest intensity) and write it down.

Let's start tapping:

Set-Up Statement: Even though I have this (intensity number) feeling because I have this limiting belief surrounding the affirmation I want to believe, I deeply and completely accept myself and how I feel.

Set-Up Statement: Even though I have this (intensity number) feeling in my (where in your body) when I say this affirmation and it makes me feel (emotion), I deeply and completely accept myself and how I feel.

Set-Up Statement: Even though I have this (emotion) feeling in my (where in your body) whenever I say that affirmation and I think the opposite, I deeply and completely accept myself and how I feel.

EB: This (emotion) feeling when I say the affirmation.
SE: This uncomfortable belief that sits underneath it.
UE: I didn't realize that I had such a limiting belief that surrounded this affirmation.
UN: This (emotion) feeling that I have not wanted to acknowledge.
CHIN: This intense feeling of (emotion) around this affirmation.
CB: This intense feeling of (emotion).
UA: I wondered why these affirmations didn't work for me.
TH: This feeling that they don't work for me.

See if you can link any patterns or memories around why the affirmation didn't work, and what was underpinning it. (If not, just continue tapping on the feeling.)

Repeat one more time and then take a deep breath and measure the level of intensity in your body.

Once you are happy that the level of emotion has dropped to a 2-0 you can begin the Reframe Round.

Reframe Reclaim Round

Start by placing your hands on your heart, and breathing slowly. Breathe in all the energy of this new belief into your heart, and as you breathe out release any limiting beliefs that no longer serve you.

See if you can create a picture in your mind of creating an affirmation that resonated and felt true for you. How would you act differently, if this was already in your life? What words would you use? What actions would you take? How would you choose to spend the moments in your day?

Set-Up Statement: Even though in the past this affirmation didn't eventuate because of my belief otherwise, which is now a level (new level of intensity), I choose now to be open to the possibility that this affirmation could work for me. And I deeply and completely accept this new belief.

Set-Up Statement: Even though the limiting belief that held back the affirmation in the past has now lessened, I choose now to imagine what life would be like if I truly believed that it could work for me. And I deeply and completely accept this new reality.

Set-Up Statement: Even though I have released the limiting belief underpinning this affirmation, I choose to be open to other limiting beliefs, and I choose to reclaim the beliefs that empower me, and attract opportunities into my life in many ways. And I deeply and completely accept this new belief.

EB: I choose to allow myself to imagine what life would be like if this affirmation were true.

SE: I choose to release any and all self-imposed limiting beliefs surrounding this affirmation.

UE: I choose to allow myself to believe it could possibly be true.

UN: I choose to be open to all the possibilities that allow the energy to flow into my life.

CHIN: I choose to allow ideas and inspiration to flow.

CB: I am now grateful for this affirmation and the way it helps me be open to accepting all the ways in which opportunities show up in my life.

UA: I am so grateful for the knowledge that shows up in my life every day in many ways.

TH: I choose to embrace this way of being in all aspects of my life.

The Power Pose

Now stand with your hands on your hips, feet slightly apart (you can do this physically, or just imagine yourself doing it). Imagine that you are standing in the most powerful position you can. Your shoulders are back, your back is straight.

Create a powerful affirmation that resonates with you, perhaps choosing a statement from the *reframe* round.

Imagine that you are drawing up all the confidence, power, and energy of this new belief that you need through your feet and up into your heart. Then imagine that all that new energy is being distributed to every cell in your body. Hold this pose (or the image of this pose) for about 1 to 2 minutes, until you can feel this new energy powering in your body.

CHAPTER 24

Tapping on the Fear of Disappointing Others

Often when we create an intention for what we want, there are others involved in the success. For example, your financial success may dictate what you can do for your family; or perhaps losing weight will impact on how you can spend time with your children doing the activities they want.

However, sometimes the intention can also harbor a fear of disappointing others. That fear then can be enough to create excuses and sabotage your success and cause you to walk away from what you want. It may feel safer to avoid the disappointment that others will experience, rather than succeeding.

Margie's Story

When Margie came to see me she really felt stuck. She had been running a small online business for a number of years but she just couldn't seem to get it to a point where it could support her family.

Her husband was a builder. While he had some great years, one of the projects he was working on recently was placed into voluntary liquidation. It meant almost a year of their income was held up and there was a chance that he would not be paid at all.

So while Margie's husband was going through incredible feelings of anger and self-doubt, Margie felt that she could really get her business to a point where it could support the family. But she had this nagging fear that just seemed to hold her back.

"I know I can do this," she said, "but what if I can't? There seems to be something that is just blocking me from stepping up. I have done this before you know. I have started a couple of businesses in the past, and I had all great expectations and dreams about what I wanted to do, but I just couldn't deliver. *Aggh,* this is so annoying! How can I want something so badly, but not achieve it?"

First we tapped on the feeling of wanting something badly and not achieving it. I asked her to create a picture of what she really wanted – a big *stretch* goal.

She said, "I want to get my business to the point where it makes $250,000 a year."

I then asked her to look at that statement and write down all the feelings that came up for her, without judging the feelings or editing. Just put the pen to paper and write.

It didn't take her long to come up with a long list.

1. *What if I can't do it?*
2. *I hate people relying on me.*
3. *What if I stuff it up?*
4. *What if I can't deliver what they want?*
5. *What if I fail?*
6. *All this expectation on my shoulders, what if I disappoint them?*

7. *I feel so much responsibility.*
8. *What if I am all talk and no action?*
9. *Sometimes it's better to not do it than to fail.*

I asked Margie to look at the list that she wrote and pick one that had the most emotion around it.

"There are two," she said. "The one about *what if I can't deliver what they want*, and also *all this expectation, what if I disappoint them?*"

I asked Margie if there was a time she could remember where she felt that there was all this expectation on her and she felt she had disappointed someone.

At first, she couldn't think of anything so we just started tapping on the words: *All this expectation. What if I disappoint them?*

After a round of tapping, she suddenly started looking to the left. This was an indication to me that a memory from her past was starting to surface. Our eyes are a dead giveaway. Often looking to the left is a memory of the past and looking to the right is a fear or concern about the future.

I asked her if she remembered something.

"I do," she said. "I was in Year 8 at school, I think I was 14. My parents had seven children, all of us in Catholic schools. Year 8 was called a scholarship year. We could sit for a scholarship to help with school fees. I remember that it was the princely sum of about $30 or something, but it was a pretty big deal back then. My parents were really hoping I would get a scholarship because it would have really helped them. I actually don't think they ever said anything to me, but I could feel the expectation on me to get the scholarship. For some reason, the scholarship recipients were announced at an assembly where the parents were in attendance. My name wasn't called. I remember the look in my mother's eyes, she was so disappointed!

"What was worse was that I had been an excellent student in primary school, always in the top ten in my class. I don't know what happened in high school, but it's like all the wheels fell off, I just struggled. But when I think about it now you know, I didn't even study for that exam, and I just expected that I would get it. Oh wow, I can feel the guilt and the disappointment; I knew I hadn't done enough, I just expected to get it."

As we tapped on the memory, Annie began to cry. "I feel so sad for my parents, you know? They really struggled with money to put us all through school. I could have easily had gotten that scholarship, but I didn't even study for it; I just expected I would get it. I could have done it, but I let everybody down – all that expectation and I let my parents down."

The more we tapped on each of the emotions Annie felt, the more she could see how the pattern played out in her life. Every time she felt the expectation of being responsible for bringing money into the family, she froze, the fear of failing and disappointing others stopping her from moving forward. She could also see this pattern of just expecting others to fill the gap.

"I have done this all my life. I say what I want, set these huge goals and intentions, then when it's my turn to walk the walk, I back away! I am so fearful of disappointing others, I just stop. Then I just expect someone like my husband to step up and rescue me. Oh gosh, that's it. That's the pattern!"

Whenever there is doubt, fear, or a pattern in our lives that stops us achieving that intention we want, there is *always* a reason. Our challenge is to be open to the feelings; to not ignore them, but to go deep within to find the reason, the pattern, the thought, or the belief.

So many times we think our patterns are us. They are not. Over and over again I see this, not only for my clients but in my own life. Whenever something occurs more than once – it's a pattern. It's not you – it's just a pattern, based on an event that created a belief about you.

You can change that, and your life, by simply changing the underlying belief that created the pattern in the first place.

When you do that ... the opportunities are limitless!

Tapping on Fear of Disappointing Others

For this exercise, look at your intention and make it as big as possible. While looking at it, imagine how this intention would impact on those important people in your life if you don't achieve it.

Is there fear about telling others in case you don't achieve it? Is there expectation? Is there an overwhelming feeling of responsibility? Do you feel that if you don't achieve this, you would be letting others down?

Next, try to *feel* where the emotion is in your body. Is it in your stomach? Your heart? Your head? Then measure the level of intensity on a scale of 1-10 (10 being the highest intensity) and write it down.

Let's start tapping:

Set-Up Statement: Even though I have this (intensity number) feeling because I am scared that if I don't achieve this I will let others down, I deeply and completely accept myself and how I feel.

Set-Up Statement: Even though I have this (intensity number) feeling in my (where in your body) about letting others down if I don't achieve this and it makes me feel (emotion), I deeply and completely accept myself and how I feel.

Set-Up Statement: Even though I have this (emotion) feeling in my (where in your body) whenever I think about letting others down and all these feelings of responsibility, I deeply and completely accept myself and how I feel.

EB: This (emotion) feeling.

SE: This responsibility.

UE: What if I let them all down?

UN: This (emotion) feeling of responsibility and expectation.

CHIN: This intense feeling of (emotion) because what if I don't achieve it?

CB: This intense feeling of (emotion).

UA: I just am not sure I want all this responsibility to succeed.

TH: What if I let everybody down?

See if you can link any patterns or memories around responsibility or letting others down. (If not, just continue tapping on the feeling.)

Repeat one more time and then take a deep breath and measure the level of intensity in your body.

Once you are happy that the level of emotion has dropped to a 2-0 you can begin the Reframe Round.

Reframe Reclaim Round

First hold your hands over your heart.

Breathing in slowly and out slowly, see if you can create a picture in your mind of this new reality of confidence. How would you act differently if you believed that you would not let people down? What words would you use? What actions would you take? Who would you spend time with? How would you choose to spend the moments in your day? Your subconscious does not know the difference between what is reality now and what is yet to be reality.

Set-Up Statement: Even though I had this uncomfortable feeling, which is now a level (new level of intensity), I choose now to trust that I am perfectly capable of achieving what I want. And I deeply and completely accept this new belief.

Set-Up Statement: Even though the uncomfortable feeling is no longer a strong feeling, I choose now to imagine what life would be like if I knew I could do this, and I deeply and completely accept this new belief in me.

Set-Up Statement: Even though I have released the intensity of feeling responsible, I choose to be open to other limiting beliefs, and I choose to reclaim the beliefs that empower me, and attract opportunities into my life in many ways. And I deeply and completely accept this new belief.

EB: I choose to allow myself to feel confident to achieve what I want in the right time.

SE: I choose to release any and all self-imposed limiting beliefs about letting others down.

UE: I choose to allow myself to feel empowered and able.

UN: I choose to be open to all the possibilities that come by releasing the burden of expectation of others.

CHIN: I choose to allow ideas and inspiration to flow.

CB: I am now grateful for this new way of thinking about myself.

UA: I am so grateful for the excitement I now feel in achieving my intentions.

TH: I choose to embrace this way of being in all aspects of my life.

The Power Pose

Now stand with your hands on your hips, feet slightly apart (you can do this physically, or just imagine yourself doing it). Imagine that you are standing in the most powerful position you can. Your shoulders are back, your back is straight.

Create a powerful affirmation that resonates with you, perhaps choosing a statement from the *reframe* round.

Imagine that you are drawing up all the confidence, power and knowledge you need through your feet and up into your heart. Then imagine that all that new energy is being distributed to every cell in your body. Hold this pose (or the image of this pose) for about 1 to 2 minutes, until you can feel this new energy powering in your body.

CHAPTER 25

Fear of the Light of Success

In Chapter 6, we talked about self-sabotage and how we create what author Gay Hendricks calls *our upper limit* problem, the very real excuses we make for ourselves that hold us back from experiencing success.

Upper limit problems often appear when we feel unsafe in stepping into our intentions; when the fear of who we are about to become overrides the desire to actually achieve what we want.

In my work with clients I am seeing one pattern in particular (one that was also my own) and that is the fear of stepping into the light of our own success.

Success can be a lonely, isolating place. It is truly the road less travelled. Why? Because the path to success is a bumpy, steep, and uncharted path. The Google map of our journey never takes the easy path to success, and it's why so few people achieve it. I have yet to meet a successful person, whether that be in career, money, relationships, or even weight, who has not experienced incredibly challenging times in their lives; when their belief in themselves is very often the *only* resource they have.

That path to success will challenge the very core of what you believe about yourself, and will require you to do one thing in particular – and that is to step into your true self. Allow your light to shine and be who you are really meant to be.

But for many people, shining that light can be terrifying because it means being *who* you are truly meant to be. To release the person you have created to protect you from that light, so you don't get hurt.

You see, being mediocre means you travel under the radar. You dim your light so that others can't criticize, characterize, or drag you down. In my experience, in working with many successful women, taking the leap from fairly safe and comfortable mediocrity and moving into true success is fraught with so many fears.

The unspoken anxiety-ridden fear that wakes you up at 2am most often causes us to stay right where we are. We are frozen, immobilized, and unable to move right into our light, because that means we may be vulnerable. *What if I can't maintain this? What if I fail? I am not pretty enough or slim enough to do this. Other people are smarter than me. What if they criticize me? What if they find out I am a fraud?*

Since I began tapping, I can now see so many times in my life when I was so close to success that it scared me, so I backed away. I made excuses or sabotaged myself in some way – even to the point of manifesting injury or illness. This was safer than stepping into the light of my true self and my true success because if I failed at what I truly loved to do, the pain would be far greater than being successful at something that was not connected to my heart and soul.

In any career I worked in, I always rose very quickly to success. Carving a career sometimes out of nothing, seeing opportunities that other people were not taking, saying yes to projects without having a clue how I was going to pull them off, but knowing I would always find a way. I was the perfect employee because I would work the hours, find the solution, and excel over and above what was expected of me. It was easy too, because in a *job* it wasn't really me. It was something I was doing for others. So while I was excelling and good at what I did, it wasn't about me, it wasn't about my passion, it wasn't about the *who* I really was. Even though I was successful, each and every day there was a little piece of me dying inside.

When I started teaching aerobics, way back in 1980, I quickly carved a niche and rose very quickly through the ranks. Gerry and I opened aerobic studios in brand new locations; I wrote an Instructor Training program because there wasn't one; I starred in a cable fitness TV show, because there wasn't one; and finally, I hosted an enormous indoor aerobic class with over 2,000 participants ... because it had never been done before.

But then, I created an *upper limit* problem. I was too exposed. I wasn't pretty enough, I wasn't thin enough, and I didn't have long skinny legs like other instructors. What if they found out I was a fraud? What if they found out I wasn't as good as they thought I was? All those thoughts and fears that would wake me up at 2am, terrified of the prospect. What if I failed? It would be too painful – walking away and pretending it didn't matter was far safer than shining my light and having it taken away from me.

When I wrote my first book, *David's Gift*, the same thing happened. It took me a year to write it. I would stress over the littlest thing, agonize over the layout, the cover, the way in which I wrote it. All the while worrying that it wasn't good enough – that I wasn't good enough.

Then the same thing happened. It became an overnight success. We managed to get on two national shows and various radio talk shows. But again, I backed away, made excuses, stressed about strategy and systems. It was really only fear. I was fearful of being criticized, not feeling good enough. Even though the book was a huge success, I struggled with the new place I was in. Any small amount of negative feedback would send me into weeks of questioning myself and my abilities.

It was only when I discovered tapping that I discovered what the problem was for me. I was terrified of stepping into my own success. The light actually scared me; the possibilities were overwhelming; the *what ifs* were just too confronting to even contemplate. But it all came down to one incident that happened when I was ten years old. When I was asked to sing in front of the whole school and I froze. I now know it was from the overwhelming stress that I couldn't sing, and people laughed at me.

That one moment impacted on my life for over 40 years. The memory of my friends laughing at me and people criticizing me was enough for the amygdala in my brain to send out early warning signals, every time I was about to step into the bright light again. The fear of criticism and ridicule was too painful. My 10-year-old self had nobody to talk to. Nobody to tell her that it was okay, to tell me that it wasn't that I wasn't talented, it was just that I was too nervous. There was probably nobody to tell me that, because I didn't say anything. But that fear, embarrassment, and disappointment was enough to send out the early warning signals, every single time I was doing something that I was passionate about.

I wouldn't be writing this book today if I hadn't tapped on all the moments in my life when there was an issue around shining my light. Tapping on all the times I was told: "What makes you think you are so special?" "Don't be too successful, because people will try to knock you down." "Always remember where you came from." "Why do you think you are so clever?" "Who do you think you are?"

The power of each of those phrases reaffirmed the fear held trapped in the amygdala of my brain and reminded me that showing my true passion to the world is a frightening, scary, embarrassing, painful, dangerous thing to do.

It is why, each and every day, I am so incredibly grateful for this wonderful technique that frees you from the self-imposed limitations that start with an event, a person, or words that cause you pain. That pain then creates beliefs of limitations, and patterns that continually play themselves out. Those patterns change the direction of your life – and dim the light that is truly yours to shine.

Tapping on Feeling Safe to Shine Your Light

To begin, measure the *feeling* in your body when you ask the questions:

"Do I feel safe to shine?" "Do I fear success?" "Is there a part of me that feels scared to be successful?" "When in the past have I felt unsafe to be really me?"

Next, try to feel where the emotion is in your body. Is it in your stomach? Your heart? Your head? Then measure the level of intensity on a scale of 1-10 (10 being the highest intensity) and write it down.

Let's start tapping:

Set-Up Statement: Even though I have this (intensity number) feeling because I feel fear around my own success, I deeply and completely accept myself and how I feel.

Set-Up Statement: Even though I have this (intensity number) feeling in my (where in your body) about really stepping into my own light, and it makes me feel (emotion), I deeply and completely accept myself and how I feel.

Set-Up Statement: Even though I have this (emotion) feeling in my (where in your body) whenever I think about being really being successful at what I love to do, I deeply and completely accept myself and how I feel.

EB: This (emotion) feeling.

SE: This fear.

UE: This fear of shining my light.

UN: This (emotion) feeling of being exposed and unsafe.

CHIN: This intense feeling of (emotion) because *what if I am criticized?*

CB: This intense feeling of (emotion).

UA: What if I am not really good enough?

TH: This overwhelming feeling of fear of stepping into my true light.

See if you can link any patterns or memories around being criticized or feeling unsafe when you were doing, or wanted to do, something you truly loved to do. (If not, just continue tapping on the feeling.)

Repeat one more time and then take a deep breath and measure the level of intensity in your body.

Once you are happy that the level of emotion has dropped to a 2-0 you can begin the Reframe Round.

Reframe Reclaim Round

First hold your hands over your heart.

Breathing in slowly and out slowly, see if you can create a picture in your mind of a new reality of living on purpose and living in the light of success. How would you act differently, if this was already in your life? What words would you use if you felt safe to be successful? What actions would you take? Who would you spend time with? How would you choose to spend the moments in your day? Your subconscious does not know the difference between what is reality now and what is yet to be reality.

Set-Up Statement: Even though I had this uncomfortable feeling, which is now a level (new level of intensity), I choose now to step into my own success, what I truly love to do. And I deeply and completely accept this new belief.

Set-Up Statement: Even though the uncomfortable feeling is no longer a strong feeling, I choose now to imagine what life would be like if I was living my true purpose and passion, and I deeply and completely accept this new belief in me.

Set-Up Statement: Even though I have released the intensity of the fear, I choose to be open to other limiting beliefs, and I choose to reclaim the beliefs that empower me and attract opportunities into my life in many ways. And I deeply and completely accept this new belief.

EB: I choose to allow myself time to feel successful.

SE: I choose to release any and all self-imposed limiting beliefs about myself and my success.

UE: I choose to give myself permission to shine.

UN: I choose to be open to all the possibilities that present themselves with my perfect opportunities.

CHIN: I choose to give myself permission to be all I can be.

CB: I am now grateful for the opportunities that allow me to be successful in my life.

UA: I am so grateful for this new found confidence and light.

TH: I choose to embrace this way of being in all aspects of my life.

The Power Pose

Now stand with your hands on your hips, feet slightly apart (you can do this physically, or just imagine yourself doing it). Imagine that you are standing in the most powerful position you can. Your shoulders are back, your back is straight.

Create a powerful affirmation that resonates with you, perhaps choosing a statement from the *reframe* round.

Imagine that you are drawing up all the confidence, power, and knowledge you need through your feet and up into your heart. Then imagine that all that new energy is being distributed to every cell in your body. Hold this pose (or the image of this pose) for about 1 to 2 minutes, until you can feel this new energy powering in your body.

CHAPTER 26

Trusting and Believing Even When Things go Wrong

There can be a tendency on this journey of intention setting, tapping, meditation, and visioning to be pulled off course when something goes wrong.

Life is full of wonderful times, but life can also have its challenges.

I have often had tearful phone calls from clients who say, "I am doing all the right things. I am tapping, I am meditating, journaling, and staying focused, but THIS just happened ... what's going on?"

My simple response is just one word – *life*! The wondrous, challenging, glorious, frustrating, beautiful, annoying presence we all live every day, called *life*.

As I am writing this chapter today, I actually had a number of other plans. I had a *to do* list a mile long in preparation for a *Reclaim You* event tomorrow morning, but I had also organized to meet up with a colleague at 9am to talk about plans for programs for next year. So this morning, I skipped my workout to fit in some writing and other things before meeting her and then I could head off to purchase what I needed for the event.

I drove my car to the service station to get some petrol, paid for it, jumped back in the car and it wouldn't start. My husband came to meet me with some jumper leads thinking it was simply a flat battery. Once we'd pushed it away from the pumps we hooked up the leads – and it still didn't start.

So we contacted our auto electrician, organized the towing of the car, drove back home, and here I am back at my desk 90 minutes later – rescheduling plans for the day.

There was a part of me that wanted to get truly frustrated and annoyed and stressed. But I know now with tapping and all the self-development work I have done over the past 35 years, that getting angry or frustrated is not going to create an outcome.

Did I want to get angry? Yes! Did I want to yell at the Universe and say, "What the heck, what is this all about?" Yes! Would it do any good? No!

It is all well and good to believe that staying focused and using visualization, tapping, or meditation works in the good times; it's when things feel as if they are going pear-shaped that you absolutely need to walk the walk, and talk the talk.

It is right there in those moments that all the work you have done up until that point swings into action. I just believe that no matter what, no matter what challenges are delivered, I will always find a solution. Because that is the place I live in; no matter how challenging, there will always be a solution – and often times hours, days, weeks, or months later I will figure out *why* it happened.

All your *Higher Self* needs is for you to keep up your 50% of the bargain and it will provide the alternative solutions. When you fall into stress, anxiety, frustration, or anger, your stress response kicks into the flight, fight, or freeze response and you can't think clearly.

Life's challenges are always an opportunity to learn more about you, revisit any disempowering beliefs you still have, and constantly focus on clearing any lingering energy that pulls you out of focus. It's just that simple.

But right there, in that frustrating moment when things do not go right, is the time that you also:

a. Have the most power.
b. Will realize what beliefs about yourself you still haven't cleared.

Recently I was talking to a client who is going through some challenges. She had separated from her husband, and was having problems with one of her managers from work who seemed to make her life hell. Added to her stress was the fact that her mum had recently been admitted to hospital for heart problems. One day as she was leaving for work, her son slammed the glass sliding door and the pane of glass fell out of the frame, shattering everywhere. He wasn't hurt, but the clean-up was massive and she had to call work and tell them she would be late, while waiting for the door to be repaired.

She phoned me in tears and said, "Why does this always happen to me? I am doing all the right things. How come no matter how much I am focused, how much I believe in the power of the Universe, something always happens to me!"

So the first thing I asked her was, "When has this happened to you before?"

She responded, "All the damn time!"

"OK" I said, "but can you remember a time when that first happened to you?"

I could hear the audible groan through the phone! "Not this again?" she said.

Every time you say, "This happens to me all the time," then it is a pattern. There is somewhere deep within you where you believe that no matter how much you try, something or somebody will get in the way to cause you frustration.

"But it's not my stuff," she said.

"Oh yes it is!" was my response.

You are 50% responsible for *everything* that happens in your life, because you are responsible for how you choose to see it.

Nobody can make you frustrated: only you can.

Nobody can make you angry: only you can.

Nobody can make you stressed, pissed off, annoyed, heartbroken. Nobody – only you can.

We are totally in charge of how we see our lives and how we respond.

So I asked her again, "Can you think of a time when you felt that no matter how hard you tried, something happened and you couldn't get what you wanted?"

She took a deep breath and I asked her to just start tapping. After a few moments she said, "You know, I have just had the funniest memory. I remember when I was, I don't know, about 4 or 5 years old and my grandfather had given us some money to go to the store to buy something, I think it was like 50c or something, but I remember that it was a pretty big deal, because my parents didn't have much money.

"So we went to the store and I took ages to decide what to buy. I remember the store. It was one of those old-fashioned corner stores, where the sweets were all laid out in glass bottles on the counter. My big brother chose his sweets pretty quickly and he was getting really annoyed because I was taking so long.

"Finally I decided on the sweets I wanted and I remember walking out of the store. It had those multi-colored strips that hang down from the doorway – must have been to keep the flies out or something. Anyway, as I walked through those strips, it had started to rain and I tripped up, and as I did, my bag of sweets fell out of my hand, and went into the large drain!

"I can still remember lying on the ground; I was all wet, and my brother was trying to help me to grab the sweet packet out of the drain but it was too late, they were gone. I was so upset, and even though he shared some of his with me, they weren't what I wanted. No matter how much I tried I couldn't get what I wanted!"

As we tapped on the memory, other memories of other times in her life also popped in her mind. Finally she said, "You know, I say that all the time: *No matter how hard I try I never get what I want or something always happens to me* – and of course it always does! Talk about self-fulfilling prophecy!"

We are the masters of our own responses. The next time you find yourself saying, "This always happens to me," or "Nothing I ever do works anyway," – stop and try to recall *When did you start saying them?* See if you can link them to a time in your life where something happened. Check to make sure it's not a generational pattern – something your mother or your father used to say all the time, which you have just inherited.

Our words reflect what we believe to be true about ourselves and our lives – if you don't like your current reality, change the words you use and see if it makes a difference.

When challenges arrive in your life you may not be able to control them – but you have control over how you handle them. And that can make all the difference. Your *Higher Self* will never abandon you. It will just wait patiently until you get back in flow again!

Tapping for When Things go Wrong

This tapping script is for when things always seem to go wrong, or when you feel as if things *always happen to you!*

Now measure the *feeling* in your body when you make the statement, "This always happens to me."

Is it confusion? Is it frustration? Is it fear? Is it sadness? Is it a sense of, *what's the point?*

Next, try to *feel* where the emotion is in your body. Is it in your stomach? Your heart? Your head? Then measure the level of intensity on a scale of 1-10 (10 being the highest intensity) and write it down.

Let's start tapping:

Set-Up Statement: Even though I have this (intensity number) feeling because things feel like they are just going wrong, I deeply and completely accept myself and how I feel.

Set-Up Statement: Even though I have this (intensity number) feeling in my (where in your body) because I feel that nothing is working for me right now, and it makes me feel (emotion), I deeply and completely accept myself and how I feel.

Set-Up Statement: Even though I have this (emotion) feeling in my (where in your body) because I just feel it's all too hard, I deeply and completely accept myself and how I feel.

EB: This (emotion) feeling.
SE: This frustrating feeling.
UE: Nothing is working right now.
UN: This frustration and stress about things I can't control.
CHIN: This intense feeling of (emotion) because it feels like this always happens to me.
CB: This intense feeling of (emotion).
UA: I feel so stressed and frustrated.
TH: This overwhelming feeling of things being out of my control.

See if you can link any patterns or memories around the thought *this always happens to me* or *things always go wrong*. (If not, just continue tapping on the feeling.)

Repeat one more time and then take a deep breath and measure the level of intensity in your body.

Once you are happy that the level of emotion has dropped to a 2-0 you can begin the Reframe Round.

Reframe Reclaim Round

Start by placing your hands on your heart, and breathing slowly. Breathe in all the energy of forgiveness into your heart, and as you breathe out release any anger or resentment that no longer serves you.

Imagine a new you by releasing and forgiving the frustration and stress of things not going well in your life. You are rewiring your beliefs, thoughts, and your actions to reflect what you want in your life. That includes acting as if it is already here!

Set-Up Statement: Even though it feels like things haven't been going well, but the frustration and stress had dropped to a level (new level of intensity), I choose now to trust that everything will work out in the right way in the right time. And I deeply and completely accept this new belief.

Set-Up Statement: Even though this frustration and stress is no longer a strong feeling, I choose now to get back in flow, and trust my innate wisdom and intuition to create a solution, and I deeply and completely accept this new belief in me.

Set-Up Statement: Even though I have released the intensity of feeling like this always happens, I choose to be open to other limiting beliefs, and I choose to reclaim the beliefs that empower me, and attract opportunities into my life in many ways. And I deeply and completely accept this new belief.

EB: I choose to allow myself to stay *in flow.*

SE: I choose to release any and all feelings of frustration and stress.

UE: I choose to allow peace and calm to flow through my body.

UN: I choose to be open to all the possibilities to creating a 'better than I thought possible' outcome.

CHIN: I choose to allow peace and joy to flow in my life.

CB: I am now grateful for the way in which peace, joy, and better than I thought possible solutions are attracted to me in many ways.

UA: I am so grateful for the knowledge that shows up in my life every day in many ways.

TH: I choose to embrace this way of being in all aspects of my life.

The Power Pose

Now stand with your hands on your hips, feet slightly apart (you can do this physically, or just imagine yourself doing it). Imagine that you are standing in the most powerful position you can. Your shoulders are back, your back is straight.

Create a powerful affirmation that resonates with you, perhaps choosing a statement from the *reframe* round.

Imagine that you are drawing up all the confidence, power, and knowledge you need through your feet and up into your heart. Then imagine that all that new energy is being distributed to every cell in your body. Hold this pose (or the image of this pose) for about 1 to 2 minutes, until you can feel this new energy powering in your body.

CHAPTER 27

Tapping for When You Have no Support

No matter how old we grow there is still a part of us that needs or wants to feel that someone is in our corner – to support and believe in us, whenever we set ourselves an intention to change our world as we know it. Somebody to have on our side when our focus wavers or doubt creeps in.

Success, as we talked about in Chapter 25, can be a lonely and challenging place. We very often need support from people who have *got our backs*. For example, in an interview with podcast host Ali Brown, on her show *Glambition Radio*, Janine Allis, the founder of Boost Juice and member of the *Shark Tank* TV show, credits her husband with providing unwavering support in the three years leading up to when Boost Juice started to make a profit.

I know in my own life, the incredible unwavering support from my husband and my children is often the only thing that has kept me moving when getting my mentoring business off the ground. Even in the writing of this book, their support with editing, proofing, and providing space to write has kept the project on track, even when other things could have taken precedence.

BUT – what if you don't have that support? What if those around you do not offer unwavering belief in your ability to achieve what you want? What then?

Louisa's Story

Louisa came from a family of high academic achievers. Her three older brothers all became doctors and she also had two younger sisters, one who became an engineer and the other a software programmer.

Louisa was the child in the middle who never seemed to fit in. She didn't do well in school, although she tried really hard. She didn't do well at sports and she tried art, but it bored her. She just couldn't find anything she excelled at but that didn't stop her trying. At one stage she went to university to study psychology, but dropped out after a year as she felt that they were all crazy! She switched to studying information technology, but again found it boring and unfulfilling.

She felt as if her father, in particular, was disappointed in her. He was always coming up with things for her to study, but would choose things she didn't really want to do. It was as if he didn't know her.

When we sat down for our first clarity session (a session I do with all new clients before coming onto the *Reclaim You* program) I asked Louisa what she wanted.

In this process we start by identifying all the words you can think of that describe the 'facets' of what you want, without actually naming what it is.

She wrote:

Something that
- *Fills my heart.*
- *Helps people.*

- *Spending time with animals.*
- *Allows me to wear what I want to wear.*
- *I can make my own hours so if I want to spend a few days in the country I can.*
- *Allows me to feel free and unencumbered.*
- *Brings in enough money to pay rent and eat organic foods.*
- *Makes me feel as if I am contributing.*
- *Allows me to be out in the fresh air.*
- *Doesn't incorporate being in an office.*
- *Is different and quirky and kind of hippy. (And drives my family nuts!)*
- *Allows me to just be me.*
- *Something I can afford to buy or to do, without having to ask my parents for money, or borrow money from the bank.*

So we then took each of those items and I asked her to write down all the *tail-enders* – that came into her mind when she thought of creating a career or job out of those statements. Immediately she wrote down:

- *It just doesn't exist.*
- *You have to have a real job and wear real clothes and high heels to be important.*
- *What I want isn't important.*
- *You can't get paid to be different and quirky.*
- *You only make money if you have a degree.*
- *You will amount to nothing anyway.*
- *I will never be as good in my parents' eyes as my siblings.*
- *They think I am a loser.*
- *They think I won't amount to anything.*
- *Making money means sacrificing your freedom.*
- *I am dumb anyway so what's the point?*

After she had finished this aspect, we created a map of how each of these thoughts made her feel:

- *Frustrated*
- *Angry*
- *Never good enough*
- *Left out*
- *Ostracized*
- *Imperfect*
- *Lazy*
- *Worthless*
- *Scared*
- *Hopeless*

I then asked her to look at each of those statements and to measure when/who/what made her feel like that in the past.

She had one comment. "My entire life. I never felt as if I was as good as my brothers or sisters. I felt like my parents continually judged me, no matter what I wanted to do. In fact I remember telling my Dad that I wanted to work with animals. He responded with, 'Well I don't think you are going to ever get enough marks in school to be a vet, so why bother!'"

We then set about tapping on each of the feelings until the emotion subsided and she was able to register a 1 or a 0 feeling for each statement.

After a couple of sessions together there was a turning point. On one of our group calls, Louisa was first one on. "I am so excited," she said. "I have just found my dream business! I was at a party on the weekend and talking to a woman who owns a dog walking business. She wants to sell it, and when I told her that it sounded like my ideal job but I didn't have the money to buy it outright, she said that it was more important for her to have somebody to take over who had a passion for animals. She asked if I would come into the business now and learn it, and then I would pay her for the business over a period of months! I am so excited. It's what I just love and so I told my Mum and Dad, and you wouldn't believe what they said; they told me that they felt it was the perfect job for me and they were so excited − go figure."

What I have seen happen over and over again is that when you become absolutely crystal clear on what you want, then tap on all those self-imposed limiting beliefs that come from the negative events, people, or words we have heard while growing up, things change. *Because* you change. Your energy, your vibration, what you believe to be true about yourself changes. And subsequently it's as if the people around you sense something different.

What was interesting in Louisa's case was that in talking to her parents, her father said that he actually wanted to support her in anything she did. He felt that if he offered suggestions and pushed her into something, she might like it. But Louisa felt that he was disappointed in her. "He only wanted me to be happy," she said. "That is amazing!"

Tapping on Feeling That Nobody Supports Me

Go back and look at the intention you wrote in Chapter 4 and check to see if there is anything more specific you want to add to your intention. Then check to see if you feel totally supported in your intention. Do you feel others understand why you want to do what you do? Do you feel you have always been supported, or were there times when you felt as if you had no support?

Next, try to *feel* where the emotion is in your body. Is it in your stomach? Your heart? Your head? Then measure the level of intensity on a scale of 1-10 (10 being the highest intensity) and write it down.

Let's start tapping:

Set-Up Statement: Even though I have this (intensity number) feeling because I feel I am not supported, I deeply and completely accept myself and how I feel.

Set-Up Statement: Even though I have this (intensity number) feeling in my (where in your body) for all the times in the past where I have not felt supported, and it makes me feel (emotion), I deeply and completely accept myself and how I feel.

Set-Up Statement: Even though I have this (emotion) feeling in my (where in your body) whenever I think about the times I felt unsupported or judged, I deeply and completely accept myself and how I feel.

EB: This (emotion) feeling.

SE: I feel unsupported.

UE: I didn't realize that this feeling ran so deep.

UN: This (emotion) feeling that I feel judged and unsupported.

CHIN: This intense feeling of (emotion) feeling as if I have no support.

CB: This intense feeling of (emotion).

UA: I feel so unsupported.

TH: This overwhelming feeling of being judged and unsupported.

See if you can link any patterns or memories around being unsupported in the past. (If not, just continue tapping on the feeling.)

Repeat one more time and then take a deep breath and measure the level of intensity in your body.

Once you are happy that the level of emotion has dropped to a 2-0 you can begin the Reframe Round.

Reframe Reclaim Round

First hold your hands over your heart.

Breathing in slowly and out slowly, see if you can create a picture in your mind of how being totally supported feels. How would you act differently, if you felt supported? What words would you use? How would others react to you? Who would you spend time with? How would you choose to spend the moments in your day? Make the picture as detailed as you can.

Set-Up Statement: Even though I had this uncomfortable feeling, which is now a level (new level of intensity), I choose now to seek out those who will support my dreams. And I deeply and completely accept this new belief.

Set-Up Statement: Even though the uncomfortable feeling is no longer a strong feeling, I choose now to imagine what life would be like if I felt supported in everything I wanted, and I deeply and completely accept this new belief in me.

Set-Up Statement: Even though I have released the intensity of not feeling supported, I choose to be open to other limiting beliefs, and I choose to reclaim the beliefs that empower me and attract opportunities into my life in many ways. And I deeply and completely accept this new belief.

EB: I choose to allow myself time to feel what support feels like.

SE: I choose to release any and all self-imposed limiting beliefs about others judging me.

UE: I choose to allow ideas and opportunities to flow easily into my life.

UN: I choose to be open to all the possibilities where support could come to me in abundance.

CHIN: I choose to allow myself to feel what it feels like to be supported.

CB: I am now grateful for all the support that is flowing to me in many ways.

UA: I am so grateful for the support that shows up in my life every day in many ways.

TH: I choose to embrace this way of being in all aspects of my life.

The Power Pose

Now stand with your hands on your hips, feet slightly apart (you can do this physically, or just imagine yourself doing it). Imagine that you are standing in the most powerful position you can. Your shoulders are back, your back is straight.

Create a powerful affirmation that resonates with you, perhaps choosing a statement from the *reframe* round.

Imagine that you are drawing up all the confidence, power, and knowledge you need through your feet and up into your heart. Then imagine that all that new energy is being distributed to every cell in your body. Hold this pose (or the image of this pose) for about 1 to 2 minutes, until you can feel this new energy powering in your body.

CHAPTER 28

Tapping on Good Fear

Over the past few chapters we have been tapping to release any limiting beliefs or fears that can be holding you back from truly manifesting what you want in your life.

But getting closer to what it is we truly want can bring up a different type of fear – the one that has you feeling you are way out of your comfort zone. It's almost as if you want to jump across a small gap between two cliffs, but between you and the other side is a deep, dark ravine. Although you know it is literally just a step away, leaving the familiarity of where you are, and have always been, is almost unthinkable.

This brings us to the difference between *good* fear and *limiting* fear.

Good fear is the adrenalin that keeps us moving forward. It's the fear that drives us out of complacency; that energizes us to take risks and propels us to make decisions we have been fearful of making before.

Good fear wakes you up out of your comfort zone and fills your heart, mind, and every single cell in your body, keeping you alive, aware, and young!

But it can also be confused with *Limiting* Fear – the fear that can hold you from stepping into your sheer brilliance.

The reason I began the *Reclaim You* seminars was that I saw so many women teetering on the edge of that *good* fear, but unable to un-tether themselves from their cliff of safe living. Women working in jobs that keep them playing small, knowing they are destined for far greater things, but the fear of playing a bigger game cementing them to the safe edge.

Or women staying in relationships that were no longer emotionally or physically intimate but feeling that they do not deserve better. The safety of settling for less.

Or women who wanted to travel the world, or write a book, or lose weight, but who were tethered to the safety of where they were, not knowing how to break free.

The first time I did a professional speaking gig, it was to an audience of over 500 women. Now I had taught a fitness class to 2000 people, as well as hosting a TV show, but actually speaking for 30 minutes to a group that large was simply terrifying. When I was asked to do it, there was part of me that believed it was way past my level of expertise. I had only just started running seminars on teaching people how to eat intuitively and how bad dieting was for you – I didn't really have any formal qualifications, I just knew that it was the truth.

I hesitated to say yes, but the organizer, who was a member at the gym I worked at, was insistent and would not take no for an answer.

In the days leading up to the presentation, I would wander around the house feeling ill as I was so nervous. I wondered if I had done the right thing, questioned my value, my worth, and my qualifications and was terrified that I would be called an imposter. Gerry was amazing; he kept encouraging me, "You have all the qualifications in the world to present on this topic – you are living it, and you are teaching others how to do it!"

I procrastinated with the presentation, I got cranky with the kids, I tidied the house, cleaned the fridge, washed the floors and windows – anything that would stop me actually feeling the fear and doing the work that needed to be done.

24 hours before the presentation I was suddenly hit with a mad rush of adrenalin – I knew I had to get this presentation finished or I'd look like a total idiot on stage.

As the night came around, I was a nervous wreck (this was many years before I discovered tapping). In fact, I was so nervous I actually thought I might be physically ill. As I walked up to the podium my hands were shaking so much I was sure people could see it.

I raced through the presentation so fast – I felt I sounded like a chipmunk and no one could have possibly understood what I was saying.

But at the end of the night there was a line of people waiting to ask me questions, with comments such as: "That was one of the most powerful talks I have ever heard!" or "You just made so much sense, it was great!" or "I have made a decision right now that I will never buy one of those diet programs again!"

From that moment on, there was no going back. The fear that I felt was *good* fear, the *stretching* fear. The one that changes you so that you can't fit back into the same persona you were before.

Each and every time you rise up to the occasion and set a goal to stretch yourself, you change in your mind and in the cells of your body what you believe possible!

Tapping on Good Fear

Now go back to your original intention. Do you feel any fear around that goal? Do you feel that it is pushing you out of your comfort zone?

Next, try to *feel* where the emotion is in your body. Is it in your stomach? Your heart? Your head? Then measure the level of intensity on a scale of 1-10 (10 being the highest intensity) and write it down.

Let's start tapping:

Set-Up Statement: Even though I have this (intensity number) feeling because I feel some level of fear around this goal, I deeply and completely accept myself and how I feel.

Set-Up Statement: Even though I have this (intensity number) feeling in my (where in your body) and it makes me feel (emotion), I deeply and completely accept myself and how I feel.

Set-Up Statement: Even though I have this (emotion) feeling in my (where in your body) whenever I think about what I want, and it pushes me beyond what I believed possible for me, I deeply and completely accept myself and how I feel.

EB: This fear.
SE: This uncomfortable fear.
UE: This fear that takes me to a place I haven't experienced before.
UN: This fear that takes me out of my comfort zone.

CHIN: This intense feeling of fear because I am wondering who I have to become to obtain it.

CB: This intense feeling of fear.

UA: Do I really want to stretch myself this far?

TH: This overwhelming fear that takes me out of my comfort zone.

See if you can link any patterns or memories around setting a true stretching or scary goal before and not achieving it, or being too scared to set one at all. (If not, just continue tapping on the feeling.)

Repeat one more time and then take a deep breath and measure the level of intensity in your body.

Once you are happy that the level of emotion has dropped to a 2-0 you can begin the Reframe Round.

Reframe Reclaim Round

First hold your hands over your heart.

Breathe in slowly and see if you can create a picture in your mind of how it would feel if you simply *felt the fear and did it anyway?* How would you act differently, if you overcame this fear? What words would you use? What actions would you take? Who would you spend time with? How would you choose to spend the moments in your day? Your subconscious does not know the difference between what is reality now and what is yet to be reality.

Set-Up Statement: Even though I had this uncomfortable fear, which is now a level (new level of intensity), I choose now to be comfortable and confident in allowing myself to feel the fear and do it anyway. And I deeply and completely accept this new belief.

Set-Up Statement: Even though the uncomfortable fear is no longer a strong feeling, I choose now to imagine what life would be like if I actually achieved it, and I deeply and completely accept this new belief in me.

Set-Up Statement: Even though I have released the intensity of this fear, I choose to be open to other limiting beliefs, and I choose to reclaim the beliefs that empower me and attract opportunities into my life in many ways. And I deeply and completely accept this new belief.

EB: I choose to allow myself to expand what I believe possible for me.

SE: I choose to release any and all self-imposed limiting beliefs that have held me back before.

UE: I choose to allow myself to feel the fear, but know I can really do it if I want.

UN: I choose to be open to all the possibilities that can help me achieve this intention.

CHIN: I choose to allow ideas and inspiration to flow.

CB: I am now grateful for all the opportunities that are attracted to me in many ways.

UA: I am so grateful for the knowledge that shows up in my life every day in many ways.

TH: I choose to embrace this way of being in all aspects of my life.

The Power Pose

Now stand with your hands on your hips, feet slightly apart (you can do this physically, or just imagine yourself doing it). Imagine that you are standing in the most powerful position you can. Your shoulders are back, your back is straight.

Create a powerful affirmation that resonates with you, perhaps choosing a statement from the *reframe* round.

Imagine that you are drawing up all the confidence, power, and knowledge you need through your feet and up into your heart. Then imagine that all that new energy is being distributed to every cell in your body. Hold this pose (or the image of this pose) for about 1 to 2 minutes, until you can feel this new energy powering in your body.

CHAPTER 29

Four Generalized Tapping Scripts for the Workplace

Workplace stress now accounts for billions of dollars in lost revenue each year.

The cost of stress related illness is costing Australian business over $10 billion each year. According to a report by Safe Work Australia in 2013, mental stress claims are the most expensive form of worker's compensation claim. These claims result in workers often being absent from work for extended periods, with mental stress claims predominantly made by women.

The US claims are similar, with an article in *Forbes Magazine* quoting figures as high as $190 billion in health care costs.

Workplace stress is a serious issue.

But tapping can be a great way to relieve the immediate impact of stress by lowering cortisol levels, the hormone released in times of stress.

Regular tapping both before work, in the car on the way to work, or during the work day, can help you overcome the stress response to allow you to function more effectively in your role.

Trying to ignore stressful feelings often means you take out your stress on those closest to you after you leave work. It is not only bad for your relationships, but also impacts on your health.

Tapping in this instance can be used to take the *edge off* the stressed feelings and provide relief, allowing you to think more clearly, and will help with focus and decision-making in the work environment.

Four Generalized Tapping Scripts for the Workplace

Listed below are four generalized tapping scripts that can help deal with some of the most common issues you may face in the workplace.

While these are generalized, they are designed only to take the intensity off the overwhelming feelings you may experience in the day-to-day work environment, by helping to lower cortisol levels and subsequently decreasing the stress response.

If you are suffering with chronic stress, an experienced EFT practitioner can help you get to the root cause of why you attract the emotion into your life in the first place. When that happens your ability to deal with these issues will become more powerful and, in many cases, your levels of stress will drop dramatically.

Tapping to Release Stress

If you are feeling stressed, think about where you feel the stress in your body: Is it in your stomach; your shoulders; or your chest?

Measure the level of intensity of the stress and if you can, focus on who or what is making you feel stressed.

Breathing in slowly, see if you can create a picture in your mind of this reality and how it looks right now. How would you act differently, if you felt calm and stress free? What words would you use? How would others react to you? Who would you spend time with? How would you choose to spend the moments in your day? Make the picture as detailed as you can.

Set-Up Statement: Even though I was feeling overwhelmed and stressed, but now it is a level (new level of intensity), I choose now to breathe and allow myself to feel peaceful. And I deeply and completely accept this new belief.

Set-Up Statement: Even though the stress is no longer a strong feeling, I choose now to imagine what life would be like if I could manage my stress better, and I deeply and completely accept this new belief in me.

Set-Up Statement: Even though I have released the intensity of the stress, I choose to stay in my own flow and take one day at a time, and I deeply and completely accept myself and how I feel.

EB: I choose to allow myself time to release stress as I feel it overwhelming me.
SE: I choose to stay in the present moment and in my own power.
UE: I choose to breathe and allow this stress to just leave my body.
UN: I choose to stay in the present moment.
CHIN: I choose to breathe and allow my body to release stress.
CB: I choose to release the stress from my body.
UA: I choose to honor and embrace all support I may not have seen yet.
TH: I choose to embrace this way of being in all aspects of my life.

The Power Pose

Now stand with your hands on your hips, feet slightly apart (you can do this physically, or just imagine yourself doing it). Imagine that you are standing in the most powerful position you can. Your shoulders are back, your back is straight.

Create a powerful affirmation that resonates with you, perhaps choosing a statement from the *reframe* round.

Imagine that you are drawing up all the confidence, power, and knowledge you need through your feet and up into your heart. Then imagine that all that new energy is being distributed to every cell in your body. Hold this pose (or the image of this pose) for about 1 to 2 minutes, until you can feel this new energy powering in your body.

Tapping to Release Overwhelm

If you are feeling overwhelmed, think about where you feel the overwhelm feeling in your body: Is it in your stomach; your shoulders; or your chest?

Measure the level of intensity of the feeling of overwhelm and if you can, focus on who or what is making you feel that way.

Let's start tapping:

Set-Up Statement: Even though I have this (intensity number) overwhelm in my body, I deeply and completely accept myself and how I feel.

control of the situation? What words would you use? How would others react to you? Who would you spend time with? How would you choose to spend the moments in your day? Make the picture as detailed as you can.

Set-Up Statement: Even though I was feeling overwhelm, but now it is a level (new level of intensity), I choose now to breathe and allow myself to feel calm and release the overwhelming feeling. And I deeply and completely accept this new feeling.

Set-Up Statement: Even though the overwhelm is no longer a strong feeling, I choose now to imagine what life would be like if I could release the feeling of being overwhelmed, and I deeply and completely accept this new feeling in me.

Set-Up Statement: Even though I have released the intensity of this overwhelm, I choose to stay in my own flow and stay focused on completing one task at a time. And I deeply and completely accept this new feeling.

EB: I choose to allow myself time to release the overwhelm feeling and feel peace in my body.
SE: I choose to stay in the present moment and take things one step at a time.
UE: I choose to breathe and allow the overwhelm feeling to just leave my body.
UN: I choose to stay focused on doing one task at a time.
CHIN: I choose to breathe and allow my body to release this overwhelm feeling.
CB: I choose to release the overwhelm feeling from my body.
UA: I choose to honor myself and breathe through this feeling.
TH: I choose to embrace this way of being in all aspects of my life.

The Power Pose

Now stand with your hands on your hips, feet slightly apart (you can do this physically, or just imagine yourself doing it). Imagine that you are standing in the most powerful position you can. Your shoulders are back, your back is straight.

Create a powerful affirmation that resonates with you, perhaps choosing a statement from the *reframe* round.

Imagine that you are drawing up all the confidence, power, and knowledge you need through your feet and up into your heart. Then imagine that all that new energy is being distributed to every cell in your body. Hold this pose (or the image of this pose) for about 1 to 2 minutes, until you can feel this new energy powering in your body.

Tapping on Feeling You Don't Have Enough Time

If you are feeling that you just don't have enough time to do everything you are required to do, stop for moment and feel what the emotion feels like in your body and where it is: Is it in your stomach; your shoulders; or your chest?

Let's start tapping:

Set-Up Statement: Even though I have this (intensity number) of feeling I don't have enough time to do everything I need to do today, I deeply and completely accept myself and how I feel.

289

Breathing in slowly and out slowly, see if you can create a picture in your mind of how you would feel if you were in total control of your time. If you believed that time was on your side imagine what it would feel like to feel as if you could slow time down.

How would you act differently, if you had all the time in the world to achieve what you need to do? What words would you use? How would others react to you? Who would you spend time with? How would you choose to spend the moments in your day? Make the picture as detailed as you can.

Set-Up Statement: Even though I was feeling that I didn't have enough time, but now it is a level (new level of intensity), I choose now to breathe and allow myself to believe that time is always on my side. And I deeply and completely accept this new feeling.

Set-Up Statement: Even though the feeling that I don't have enough time is no longer a strong feeling, I choose now to imagine what life would be like if I truly believed that I could slow time down, and I deeply and completely accept this new feeling in me.

Set-Up Statement: Even though I have released the intensity of the feeling I won't have enough time, I choose to stay in my own flow and stay focused on completing one task at a time. And I deeply and completely accept this new feeling.

EB: I choose to allow myself time to trust that there is always enough time.

SE: I choose to stay in the present moment and take things one step at a time.

UE: I choose to breathe and allow myself to feel that I can slow time down.

UN: I choose to stay focused on doing one task at a time.

CHIN: I choose to breathe and visualize that I have plenty of time.

CB: I choose to embrace the feeling that there is always plenty of time to do what I need to do.

UA: I choose to honor myself and breathe through this feeling.

TH: I choose to embrace this way of being in all aspects of my life.

The Power Pose

Now stand with your hands on your hips, feet slightly apart (you can do this physically, or just imagine yourself doing it). Imagine that you are standing in the most powerful position you can. Your shoulders are back, your back is straight.

Create a powerful affirmation that resonates with you, perhaps choosing a statement from the *reframe* round.

Imagine that you are drawing up all the confidence, power, and knowledge you need through your feet and up into your heart. Then imagine that all that new energy is being distributed to every cell in your body. Hold this pose (or the image of this pose) for about 1 to 2 minutes, until you can feel this new energy powering in your body.

Tapping on Feeling That You Have Too Much to Do

If you are feeling that you just have way too much to do, stop for a moment and feel what the emotion feels like in your body and where it is: Is it in your stomach; your shoulders; or your chest?

Measure the level of intensity of the feeling and if you can, focus on who or what is making you feel that way.

Let's start tapping:

Set-Up Statement: Even though I have this (intensity number) of feeling that I have way too much to do today, I deeply and completely accept myself and how I feel.

Set-Up Statement: Even though I have this (intensity number) feeling that I have too much to get done today and I feel it (where in your body) and it makes me feel (emotion), I deeply and completely accept myself and how I feel.

Set-Up Statement: Even though I have this feeling that I just have too much to do and I feel it (where in your body) whenever I think about how much I have to do, I deeply and completely accept myself and how I feel.

EB: I have too much to do.
SE: This feeling that I have just too much to do.
UE: This feeling that I will never get it all done.
UN: This feeling that there is too much pressure on me.

CHIN: This intense feeling of way too much to do.

CB: This panicked feeling in my (where in your body).

UA: This feeling that I just can't get everything done.

TH: This feeling in my (where in your body) that I have nobody to help me.

See if you can link the feeling to another time when you felt you felt like you were given too much to do, and there was nobody to help you. (If not, just continue tapping on the feeling.)

Repeat one more time and then take a deep breath and measure the level of intensity in your body.

Once you are happy that the level of emotion has dropped to a 2-0 you can begin the Reframe Round.

Reframe Reclaim Round

First hold your hands over your heart.

Breathing in slowly and out slowly, imagine how you would feel if you had everything under control.

See if you can create a picture in your mind of this reality and how it looks right now. How would you act differently if you were in total control of what you do and how you approach what you need to do? What words would you use? How would others react to you? Who would you spend time with? How would you choose to spend the moments in your day? Make the picture as detailed as you can.

Set-Up Statement: Even though I was feeling that I have too much to do, but now it is a level (new level of intensity), I choose now to breathe and allow myself to look at my *to do* list with different eyes. And I deeply and completely accept this new feeling.

Set-Up Statement: Even though the feeling that I have too much to do is no longer a strong feeling, I am going to honor myself and rethink what is important today, and I deeply and completely accept this new feeling in me.

Set-Up Statement: Even though I have released the intensity of feeling like I have too much to do, I choose to stay in my own flow and stay focused on completing one task at a time. And I deeply and completely accept this new feeling.

EB: I choose to allow myself to make a decision about what is important to do today.

SE: I choose to stay in the present moment and take things one step at a time.

UE: I choose to breathe and allow myself to release things that don't need to be done.

UN: I choose to stay focused on doing one task at a time.

CHIN: I choose to breathe and allow myself to trust that what needs to get done will get done.

CB: I choose to embrace the feeling that I am not Superwoman, and I will get done what I can, and feel OK about it.

UA: I choose to honor myself and relax and stay present today.

TH: I choose to embrace this way of being in all aspects of my life.

The Power Pose

Now stand with your hands on your hips, feet slightly apart (you can do this physically, or just imagine yourself doing it). Imagine that you are standing in the most powerful position you can. Your shoulders are back, your back is straight.

Create a powerful affirmation that resonates with you, perhaps choosing a statement from the *reframe* round.

Imagine that you are drawing up all the confidence, power and knowledge you need through your feet and up into your heart. Then imagine that all that new energy is being distributed to every cell in your body. Hold this pose (or the image of this pose) for about 1 to 2 minutes, until you can feel this new energy powering in your body.

CHAPTER 30

Celebration Time!

Congratulations! You have reached the end of the process. If you have completed the 30 days of tapping, no doubt your life looks totally different now than it did 30 days ago.

I am so honored and humbled that you have allowed me to be a part of this process with you!

Now is the time to review what you have experienced over the last month.

This process is *exceptionally* important because of the *Apex effect* – where you change and shift huge limiting beliefs but forget that you have made those changes.

Go back and look at your original journal entries. What has changed? What has happened since you began? How are you thinking differently now? How are people responding differently?

Write it all down and take a moment to allow it to truly sink in. Our subconscious seeks out success, so acknowledge any small, even infinitesimal changes that you can see, and celebrate them. We are usually the hardest person on ourselves but that's what builds success – you acknowledging your success.

Having trouble? That's okay; I have a tapping script for that too!

As a recovering perfectionist, I know it can sometimes be difficult to find the success! We don't need people to criticize us – we do that just fine on our own, thank you very much. We are so focused on the big things we forget that each day we are moving so much closer to the intention.

This is one of the biggest, most challenging issues I see with many of my clients (and why I get them to journal and also write their wins and challenges in our secret Facebook group). They simply forget or skim over the small, tiny, almost invisible steps to success that they take every single day.

That's why they have me as a mentor – I never forget! I constantly remind my clients of the incredible things they achieve each and every day. Some of them are small and difficult to measure, such as committing to write in our secret Facebook group and tapping every day; setting an intention to achieve a certain intention around honoring themselves and their time; or making a commitment to choose excellence over adequacy. Each day they are making small changes to their habits, which in the long run will compound into exceptional outcomes.

One thing I remind my clients of every single week is that they are doing what the majority of the population do not – they are working on themselves. They are making choices each and every day to improve *who* they are by choosing to eat well, meditate, journal, exercise, and tap. They are taking 100% responsibility for *who* they are and their response to what life gives them. They have moved from victim mentality to empowerment. They don't talk in terms of what people do to them, rather what they can learn from the experience and what they need to clear.

That, in itself, is incredible success. When you finally realize that you are 100% in control of your life, or at the very least, 100% in control of your responses – everything changes. You are in control. You dictate what happens in your life and you are no longer a servant to life. You are the Dame, the Madame, and the Queen. You call the shots, because you know that life is simply about becoming more of you.

You have this amazing modality literally at your fingertips that you can use every single day of your life to reclaim the *who* you were destined to be, before events, people, and words got in the way.

Whenever you feel that life is throwing you a curve ball, you just need to tap on how it makes you feel and you will understand why it is in your life.

So, if you are not *feeling it yet* ... let's tap on that!

Tapping When it is Difficult to Feel Successful

For this tapping exercise, I would like you to review your intention – the one you set almost a month ago.

I would like you to measure your level of feeling successful, or how unsuccessful you feel.

Do you feel you could have done better? Do you feel the intention you set was unachievable? Have you felt this way before?

Next, try to *feel* where the emotion is in your body. Is it in your stomach? Your heart? Your head? Then measure the level of intensity on a scale of 1-10 (10 being the highest intensity) and write it down.

Let's start tapping:

Set-Up Statement: Even though I have this (intensity number) feeling because I don't feel I have achieved what I wanted to, I deeply and completely accept myself and how I feel.

Set-Up Statement: Even though I have this (intensity number) feeling in my (where in your body) about not wanting to celebrate my success because I don't feel I have achieved what I wanted, and it makes me feel (emotion), I deeply and completely accept myself and how I feel.

Set-Up Statement: Even though I have this (emotion) feeling in my (where in your body) because I find it hard to celebrate success when I don't feel I have achieved what I wanted to, and I just don't know, I deeply and completely accept myself and how I feel.

EB: This (emotion) feeling.
SE: This *letdown* feeling.
UE: How can I celebrate success, I don't feel I have achieved what I wanted.
UN: This (emotion) feeling of not being successful.
CHIN: This intense feeling of (emotion) because it's not as good as I wanted.
CB: This intense feeling of (emotion).
UA: I don't feel successful, others achieve more than me.
TH: This overwhelming feeling I just don't feel that successful.

See if you can link any patterns or memories to not feeling successful in the past, or overlooking your achievements. (If not, just continue tapping on the feeling.)

Repeat one more time and then take a deep breath and measure the level of intensity in your body.

Once you are happy that the level of emotion has dropped to a 2-0 you can begin the Reframe Round.

Reframe Reclaim Round
First hold your hands over your heart.

Breathing in slowly and out slowly, imagine how you would feel to really celebrate success.

See if you can create a picture in your mind of this reality and how it looks right now. How would you act differently, if you allowed yourself to celebrate your own success? What words would you use? How would others react to you? Who would you spend time with? How would you choose to spend the moments in your day? Make the picture as detailed as you can.

Set-Up Statement: Even though I had this uncomfortable feeling, which is now a level (new level of intensity), I choose now to really embrace and celebrate this journey I have been on. And I deeply and completely accept this new belief.

Set-Up Statement: Even though the uncomfortable feeling is no longer a strong feeling, I choose now to imagine what life would be like if I celebrated every single small achievement in my life, and I deeply and completely accept this new belief in me.

Set-Up Statement: Even though I have released the intensity of not feeling successful, I choose to be open to other limiting beliefs, and I choose to reclaim the beliefs that empower me and attract opportunities into my life in many ways. And I deeply and completely accept this new belief.

EB: I choose to allow myself to celebrate success regularly.
SE: I choose to release any self-imposed restrictions on celebrating success.
UE: I choose to allow success to flow into my life in many ways.
UN: I choose to be open to all the possibilities for me to feel successful.

CHIN: I choose to teach my body what it feels like to be successful – just being me.

CB: I am now grateful for all the ways success shows up in my life every day.

UA: I am so grateful for the opportunity to experience success and celebrate it.

TH: I choose to embrace this way of being in all aspects of my life.

The Power Pose

Now stand with your hands on your hips, feet slightly apart (you can do this physically, or just imagine yourself doing it). Imagine that you are standing in the most powerful position you can. Your shoulders are back, your back is straight.

Create a powerful affirmation that resonates with you, perhaps choosing a statement from the *reframe* round.

Imagine that you are drawing up all the confidence, power, and knowledge you need through your feet and up into your heart. Then imagine that all that new energy is being distributed to every cell in your body. Hold this pose (or the image of this pose) for about 1 to 2 minutes, until you can feel this new energy powering in your body.

CHAPTER 31

... and Finally

Before we come to a close, there are a few things that I would like to share with you.

1. Let me know what happened.

I would love you to reach out and tell me your experience with tapping. How has it worked for you? Have there been any changes to the way you look at life?

You can message me on Facebook at www.facebook.com/sallythibault

2. I would love the opportunity to work with you.

Reclaim You **Seminars** take place throughout Australia and Canada throughout the year. For details on the next seminar go to my website: www.sallythibault.com.au

Reclaim You Now is an eight-week intensive program carried out both online and in person, designed for businesswomen who want to take their success to the next level reigniting their passion, power, and purpose. It is a powerful eight weeks of road-mapping success, overcoming fears, and allowing participants to truly reclaim the WHO they really are.

For more details send me an email at sally@sallythibault. com.au and we can set up a free strategy session to determine if and how I can help you, and if you are a right fit for the program.

3. Are you a teacher, school guidance counselor or psychologist working with school children?

Tapping in the Classroom is an interactive power-packed two-day, in-person seminar designed to help teachers and those who work with children use tapping in their classroom.

A collaboration between my dear friend Dr. Peta Stapleton and myself, the program is available in Australia, New Zealand, the US, and Canada.

For more details go to www.tappingintheclassroom.com and register for our mailing list.

4. What should you look for in an EFT practitioner?

If you are looking for an EFT practitioner to work with, there are a number of skills you should be looking for and a number of questions you can ask, to see if the practitioner is the right fit for you.

Thirty-five years ago I began working in the burgeoning, but relatively new fitness craze of aerobic dance classes. It was a wonderful time and quickly became very popular, but many people jumped on the bandwagon claiming all sorts of promises about health and losing weight that were simply not true and not substantiated. Although the fitness industry has evolved over those last 35 years, there are still products and programs that are not sustainable.

This relatively new field of EFT reminds me of that. While it has been around for many years, it is really now gaining huge worldwide attention – attracting all sorts of perceptions and variations among practitioners.

Here are a few things to look for:

i. Are they suitably qualified?

Ask where their certification comes from or if they are currently undertaking a certification process. This is a specialized modality that requires a great understanding of people and the process, something that cannot be learned from watching a few videos or taking part in a weekend seminar.

ii. Do they walk the walk?

Does the practitioner have their act together? If they specialize in the field of weight loss – are they living a healthy life? If they specialize in the area of money – are they attracting abundance in their life? If they specialize in relationships – do they have a happy, fulfilling relationship? If they specialize in success – how is that showing up in their lives? This modality is so amazing; you can simply clear any area of your life. So if you are working with a practitioner who is promising you success – and they don't have it – the warning bells need to go on!

iii. Do they practice what they preach?

In the few years I have been involved in this modality, I have met so many practitioners who never tap themselves! To me, it is the absolute essential practice in this field. You cannot work with clients unless you are living this modality yourself, otherwise you simply do not come from a place of non-judgment and clarity.

iv. Do they listen to what you say and repeat your words back to you?

A good EFT practitioner is a facilitator. In other words, they simply facilitate your own healing process. You know it is working if they are actively listening to you and repeating your words back to you, not putting words into your mouth. They should be constantly checking the level of intensity you feel the emotion, and helping you get that intensity down to a 0 if possible, or at least a level 2, before moving on to a reframe round. The sessions are about you – about ensuring that you leave feeling as if a weight has been lifted off your shoulders. Many clients talk about *feeling lighter, breathing easier*, or feeling as if the light has suddenly shifted in their world.

v. Have they explained tapping to you?

A good EFT practitioner will have a good understanding of the process and should be able to explain to you, in layman's terms, how the process will work. Make sure you feel comfortable with the practitioner and have a sense they are putting your best interests at heart.

vi. Do you feel comfortable with them?

Since I began working in this field there is one thing that I have found with good EFT practitioners … they are in no way superior nor appear to have an out-of-control ego! None! They are focused on creating the best possible outcome for their clients and they are incredibly kind, welcoming, warm, and often funny! You see, a good EFT practitioner has dealt with his or her own *stuff*. There is no pretense, no need to be anything other than *present for you*. So if you are working with a practitioner and you don't feel comfortable in their presence, or you feel they are not listening to you, keep seeking until you find the perfect fit.

A Glossary of Terms

The field of EFT has many terminologies that may be challenging to understand. Here are some explanations of the most common terms in EFT.

EFT	Emotional Freedom Techniques
Tapping	Used in reference to Emotional Freedom Techniques.
Tail-Enders	A word referring to the inner critical voice you often hear that comes from the beliefs or patterns of your past.
Aspects	An EFT term used to describe each individual piece of a larger or more *global* issue. The various issues/memories or thoughts that may support the issues around a traumatic event.
Table Tops	Referred to as a core belief.
Table Legs	The aspects that support the core belief. Memories, emotions, or feelings that support your belief.
Palace of Possibilities	Our internal world that holds all manner of possibilities.
Writing on our Walls	The people/words/events that create our belief system.

Other Phrases Used Throughout *Tapping to Reclaim You*

Intentions
Used to replace the word *goals*. Intention – a thing intended, a goal or a plan.

Manifestation
The ability to create what you focus on.

Affirmations
The assertion that something exists or is true. A statement or proposition that is declared to be true.

Your Higher Self
A terminology to describe *God, Source, Universe, The All That Is, The Dao* or *Tao*.

Co-creation
You are always creating with a source far greater than you.

Frequency Illusion
The terminology that describes how our focus shifts once we decide on something, showing up in various ways.

Confirmation Bias
The tendency to search for, interpret, favor, and recall information in a way that confirms one's beliefs or hypotheses, while giving disproportionately less consideration to alternative possibilities.

Research and References for Further Reading

Breaking the Habit of Being Yourself: How To Lose Your Mind and Create a New One
Author – Dr. Joe Dispenza
www.drjoedispenza.com

Dr. Peta Stapleton Research
www.petastapleton.com

From the Writing on Our Walls to Table Tops
Copyright – Gary and Tina Craig
www.emofree.com/eft-tutorial/tapping-deeper/writing-to-table.html

How To Want Sex Again
Author – Alina Frank
www.tapyourpower.net

Man's Search for Meaning
Author – Viktor E. Frankel
www.amazon.com/Mans-Search-Meaning-Viktor-Frankl

Mental stress costs Australian businesses more than $10 billion per year
Safe Work Australia, August 2013
MR08042013-Mental-Stress-Cost-Australian-Businesses.pdf

Secrets of a Millionaire Mind. Mastering the Inner Game of Wealth
Author – T. Harv Ecker
www.harveker.com

The Big Leap - Conquer Your Hidden Fear and Take Life to the Next Level
Author – Gay Hendricks PhD
www.hendricks.com

The Biology of Beliefs, Unleashing the Power of Consciousness, Matter and Miracles
Author – Dr. Bruce Lipton
www.brucelipton.com

The Cost of Workplace Stress In Australia
Medicare Private Report August 2008
www.medibank.com.au/client/documents/pdfs/the-cost-of-workplace-stress.pdf

The Emotional Nervous System
Author – Dr. C. George Boeree
webspace.ship.edu/cgboer/limbicsystem.html

The Tapping Solution For Weight Loss and Body Confidence
Author – Jessica Ortner
www.thetappingsolution.com

Why Tapping Works
Author – Ronald Ruben
www.lifescriptcounseling.com/research/whyitworks.pdf

Workplace Stress Responsible For Up To $190B In Annual U.S. Healthcare Costs
Forbes Magazine, 26 January 2015
http://www.forbes.com/sites/hbsworkingknowledge/2015/01/26/workplace-stress-responsible-for-up-to-190-billion-in-annual-u-s-heathcare-costs/

Your Body Language Shapes Who You Are
Amy Cuddy, TED Talk
www.ted.com/talks/amy_cuddy_your_body_language_shapes_who_you_are

Zero Limits, The Secret Hawaiian System for Wealth, Health, Peace and More
Authors – Dr. Joe Vitale and Dr. Ihaleakala Hew Len
www.zerolimits.com

Acknowledgements

Books are always a labor of love, with a loving and supportive group of individuals who help make the ideas become words and the words become a book.

My thanks to my dear friend, mentor, and tapping accountability partner Dr. Peta Stapleton, who was trailblazing this path of EFT and tapping long before it became an accepted modality. I just love our friendship – our emails, text message, phone conversations and long, long lunches, and now our collaboration on the Tapping in the Classroom Teacher training program. I am so grateful for that day I stalked you! (www.petastapleton.com and www.tappingintheclassroom.com)

To my gorgeous US friend Susan Beebe, a fellow EFT practitioner who introduced me to tapping when I thought it was a silly idea! Your expertise in sales and using this modality to help women master this often challenging aspect in business is invaluable. I so value your friendship and support. (www.tapintoyourcenter.com)

My first EFT Trainer Jenny Johnston for opening my eyes to the possibilities that EFT could open up for me. (www.jennyjohnston.com)

My beautiful best friends Kris Barrett (www.krisbarrett.com.au), Sam Gien, and Rusanne Jordan – the type of friends who you just love being with, and when the time is up you are planning when we can be together again. Thank you for reminding me every day what true friendship is really all about.

To my wonderful accountability partners Kellie Dobbie (www.transformations.com.au) and Chris Henderson (www. chrishendersoncoaching.com) for keeping me accountable to my weekly intentions!

To my gorgeous, wonderful *Reclaim You* clients who inspire me every single day to be a better EFT practitioner, facilitator, and mentor.

To my Dad, my sisters Jo, Jeannine, and Michaela, and brother Martin, who are always so supportive of the crazy ideas I have!

My editor, my cheerleader, and my daughter Alissa, whose magical eye and way with words took this sometimes rambling manuscript to a wonderful read. You are so talented my darling girl, how proud I am of you!

To Caitlin and David, my beautiful Canada-living children, who believe in the power of their dreams to make anything possible. You simply inspire me to be the best me I can be!

And finally to my twin soul and love of my life, Gerry; what a journey we have been on over the last 36 years. Thank you for constantly being there for me and supporting me to believe in a better-than-I-thought-possible outcome.

About Sally Thibault

Professional Speaker, Counselor, Author, Certified EFT
Practitioner, Mentor, and Facilitator

Businesswomen seeking to reclaim their energy, confidence, and success have a gifted mentor in Sally Thibault.

This intuitive, masterful, insightful teacher thrives on helping women overcome limiting beliefs to create success in their mind, body, relationships, and career.

Sally has worked with hundreds of women, taking powerful well-known techniques and adapting them to suit individual clients. Always with a unique feminine twist that has not been seen previously in the personal development world.

Sally's firm belief is that we are all born with our own unique feminine wisdom and intuition that can create success in our lives … and we don't have to become anybody else to do it.

Sally's own story is an inspiration in itself.

Despite failing her final Year 12 year, and being told she was not smart enough to be a teacher, Sally has spent her life teaching thousands of people to live a healthier, powerful, and more successful life.

Her career began in 1980 in the then fledgling fitness industry; teaching up to 20 hours per week; writing and facilitating one of the first fitness instructor programs; starring in her own fitness TV show; and hosting the largest indoor aerobics class with over 2,000 participants.

Sally also created one of the first fitness programs to introduce resistance work in an aerobic class. She went on to create the *Superbody* program – teaching women the art eating intuitively, releasing the diet mentality forever.

However, when Sally's son was diagnosed with autism in late 1997, her world was turned upside down. She then spent years working closely with teachers and therapists to create the best possible outcome for her son, at a time when little was known about this now persuasive condition. Her desire to teach others how to understand children living with autism led her to create a document that was widely used in the schools to help teachers work with children on the spectrum and has since been downloaded thousands of times.

Her experience led her to write the Amazon bestseller, *David's Gift: Asperger's Syndrome, Life & Love*, the inspiring true story of her family's struggles and ultimately her son's success in living with and navigating the world of autism. Her new direction began with that book, and Sally spent four years working with parents, teachers, counselors, and health professionals to understand the impact that autism has on families.

As her son grew and created his own successful life, Sally drew on her own life experiences and her qualifications in the area of fitness, health, and counseling and eventually the groundbreaking, evidence-based Emotional Freedom Techniques to create a program designed exclusively for businesswomen who want to blast the stereotypical beliefs about women, age, and success.

She created the transformational *Reclaim You* program, helping women to reignite their passion, power, and purpose to truly shine in their lives.

Sally has appeared on numerous Australian television and radio broadcasts including the *Today Show*, *The Circle*, ABC Radio, and 96.5FM Brisbane. She has also featured in many Australian newspapers and magazines such as Brisbane's *Courier Mail*, *The Gold Coast Bulletin*, *The Gold Coast Sun*, *Fitness Pro* magazine, *Healthy Life* and others. She is currently the Health and Wellness Expert on 96.5FM and Queensland Cancer Council *Live Well, Be Well* radio show.

An entertaining, informative, and powerful speaker, Sally has the ability to take challenging issues and create a transformative impact on her audience.

When Sally is not working with her clients she is spending time with her husband Gerry, chatting to her three children on Skype or Facebook, working out, or spending time with her friends drinking good champagne.

www.sallythibault.com.au

Sally invites you to join the closed Facebook group, *Tapping To Reclaim You*, for weekly videos, tips, strategies, and inspiration.

You can also connect with Sally at:
LinkedIn – au.linkedin.com/in/sallythibault
Instagram – www.instagram.com/sallythibault
Twitter – twitter.com/sallythibault

81455346R00177

Made in the USA
San Bernardino, CA
07 July 2018